Jewelry
you can make

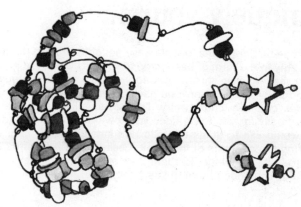

By the Editors of Sunset Books

Lane Publishing Co. • Menlo Park, California

Uniquely yours...

Ever since ancient times, people have sought to adorn themselves with things of value and beauty in the form of handmade jewelry. The case is no different today. Of course, jewelry making can sometimes require tools and techniques not readily available to the average individual. But anyone having the time and the interest can create and wear beautiful, one-of-a-kind jewelry. The projects in this book are presented in a way that makes it easy for you to produce your own unique handmade creations.

We would like to thank the following individuals for their suggestions and advice regarding the contents of this book: Leslie Correll, Charles DeCola, Nilda Duffek, William Jacquith Evans, Barbara Jee of Yarn Spectrum in Berkeley, Tidepool Gallery of Malibu, Tomnoddy Faire of Los Angeles.

Edited by Alyson Smith Gonsalves

Design: Roger Flanagan
Illustrations: Marsha Cooke
Photographs: Mona Benge
Cover: Clockwise from upper left: Trade Bead Necklace, page 24; Silver and Turquoise Belt Buckle, page 59; Rainbow's End Leather Key Ring, page 74; A Silver Ring, page 78.

Executive Editor, Sunset Books: David E. Clark
First Printing April, 1975

Contents

Jewelry: What to Make

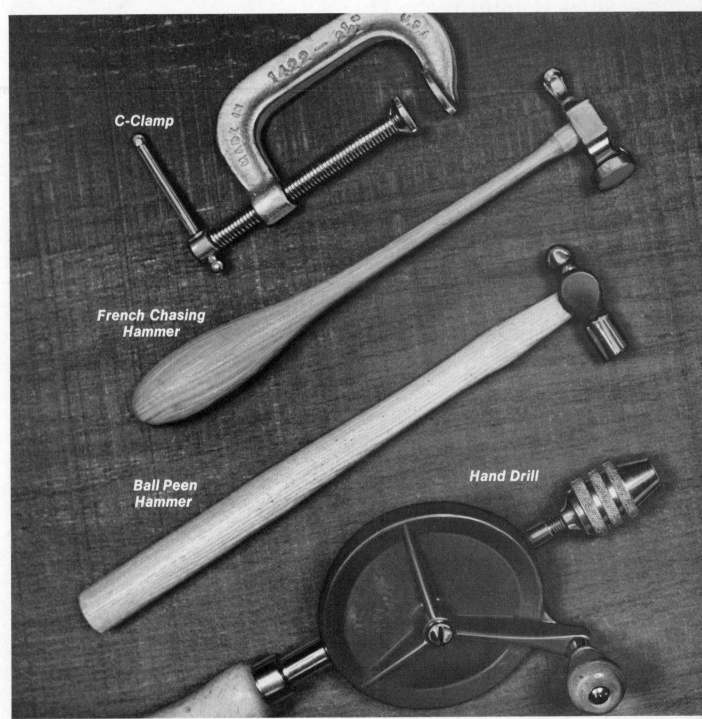

C-Clamp

French Chasing
Hammer

Ball Peen
Hammer

Hand Drill

It With

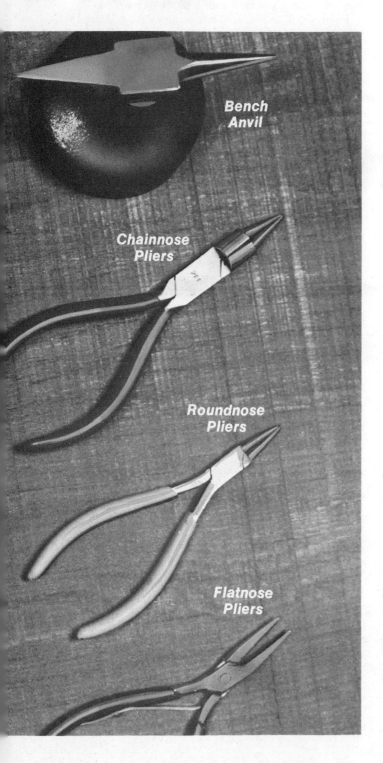

Bench Anvil

Chainnose Pliers

Roundnose Pliers

Flatnose Pliers

To learn more about the equipment and materials used to make jewelry, take a look at the following pages. Under the heading of materials, you'll find everything that has been used for the projects given in this book. You'll find information on the characteristics of each material and the uses to which the materials can be put.

There's a lot of flexibility possible in the application of materials to various designs. When you've become familiar with what's possible, feel free to stretch the limits of your imagination, adapting our suggestions to meet your own tastes.

A number of jewelry techniques require special tools. Some can be made from odds and ends or converted shop tools; other equipment must be purchased from jewelry suppliers. For an idea of the types of tools you'll need, read through this next section. We've included photos of certain pieces of equipment so you'll know what to look for when collecting the tools needed for your project. A list of jewelry suppliers is given on page 80.

A Wealth of Materials

Any item used as a part of a completed jewelry piece can be considered a material, whether it's something in its original state like wood or something finished like beads. Just about anything you can think of could qualify as a jewelry material, whether it's natural or artificial, edible or inedible. Keep your eyes open, especially around the house; you may be very surprised at what you'll find. Don't think of things only in terms of what they're supposed to be used for; invent new applications for them.

Beads: Ancient or Brand New

Beads have a special capacity to add sparkle and visual interest to any number of jewelry forms. Bead materials — such as glass, shells, paper, metal, wood, clay, plastic, fruit pits, and semiprecious stones — provide a variety of shapes, sizes, colors, and textures to choose from.

Beads may be strung together, added to such other forms as macramé, embedded in clay, combined with metal wires and cut shapes, or even sewn onto leather or cloth. Using your imagination is the most important approach to working with beads. For a look at some of the types of beads available, see the photo at upper left on the facing page.

Clays: Ceramic, Artificial, and Kitchen

Although clay can be made from a number of materials, the most common form is composed of finely ground feldspathic rock mixed with various other elements. This is the type used to make most ceramic ware. If you have access to a ceramics studio, glazes, and a kiln, feel free to use ceramic clay for all of the jewelry projects involving clay except for the finger ring on page 79.

But if you have no access to ceramics equipment, consider using one of the artificial clays available in art, hobby supply, or toy stores. These clays are usually plastic in composition and can be hardened by exposure to the air or to the heat of an ordinary oven. When dried, articles made from this clay remain somewhat flexible. As a result, they're less susceptible to breakage than items made from ceramic clay.

For an effect very similar to porcelain ceramic clay, make your own homemade "kitchen" clay. Foodstuffs used for baking are combined to make a smooth white "clay" which, when hardened by the air, closely resembles unglazed white porcelain. The recipe follows.

In a heavy enameled saucepan, combine 3 cups of baking soda, 1½ cups cornstarch, and 1¾ cups water. Stir until well blended; then turn the burner to medium heat and stir every so often until the mixture begins to thicken and bubble. Stir constantly until a doughlike consistency is reached; then turn out the mixture onto a glass or ceramic tile surface. Allow to cool slightly. Knead the clay as if kneading bread dough until a smooth, velvety dough is formed. Wrap in a damp towel and cool for ten minutes in the refrigerator. The clay is now ready to use. Since this clay dries completely when exposed to air for 24 hours, keep unused portion of clay in tightly sealed plastic bags to prevent drying out. (For ways to color the clay, see "Finishes," page 11.)

Colorful Cords and Yarns

Although color is usually added to jewelry by including bright beads or stones, it can be included less conventionally by using yarns or cords.

Cords. When stringing beads or tying sharply defined macramé knots, nothing works better than cord. To make cord, fibers such as cotton, linen, or nylon are tightly twisted and then plied or plaited together. This makes a strong, smooth-surfaced thread that has exceptional strength when waxed. It can be purchased this way, or you can wax it yourself with a block of beeswax.

Linen cord, made from exceedingly long fibers taken from the stem of the flax plant, is stronger than cotton cord, which is spun from short, twisted cotton boll fibers. Nylon cord, on the other hand, is the result of chemically produced and spun fibers that have long-wearing, elastic properties.

Any of these cords can be used for the projects in this book, and all are available in a number of colors. They are usually carried by craft or weaving supply shops; if not, check the advertising pages of any magazine dealing exclusively with crafts. They will probably contain the names and addresses of a number of sources.

Yarns. Usually spun from short fibers of both natural and synthetic materials, yarns are usually more bulky and much weaker than cord. They are best used for adding color and texture to a jewelry construction. For instant textural interest, wrap them around metal or plastic tubing, cardboard, wood shapes, or heavy clothesline.

A number of materials are used to make yarn. Wool, cotton, linen, silk, synthetics, and metallics all contribute their unique characteristics. Synthetics and metallics are made from chemically produced fibers and thin strips of colored foil; the others all come from natural sources.

Embroidery floss is another type of yarn that can be effectively used in the construction of jewelry. Made from rayon, silk, or cotton, floss is distinguished by its bright colors and silky feeling that lend a pleasing tactile effect to jewelry.

To find yarns, floss, and other related materials, check local knitting, crochet, weaving, and general needlework supply shops. Other sources may be located by consulting the advertising pages of magazines concerned with fiber crafts. For an idea of some of the kinds of cord and yarn available, see the right-hand photograph on the facing page.

Jewelry Findings: What They Are

Findings are commercially available jewelry components that are used to supplement your handmade jewelry pieces; they include clasps, metal beads, tie bars, cufflink backs, chains, earring posts and backs, jump rings, and other assorted accessories. Unless you can find an easy method for constructing the necessary findings to finish your project, they must be purchased at jewelry supply stores or from catalogue supply houses. Findings are available in a variety of metals and in a great range of sizes. You'll probably be able to get exactly the right one for your purpose. The lower left photograph on page 7 displays some of the types of findings used in jewelry making. For a list of sources, please turn to page 80.

Beads may be formed *from many materials. Those shown above include wood, eggshell, clamshell, glass, antler, clay, metal, paper, bone, seashell, ivory, semi-precious stone, and plastic.*

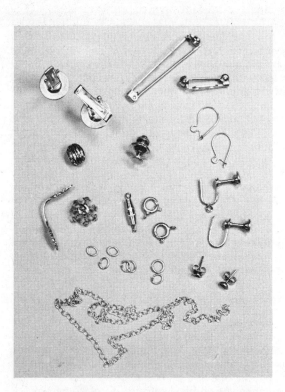

Jewelry findings, *the finishing touch for most creations, can be ordered in several precious metals or in inexpensive soft metals. Clockwise from the bottom the findings shown include: chain, jump rings, bell caps, beads, cufflink backs, pin backs, earring wires and backs, necklace clasps, and tie tack backs.*

Cords and yarns *most often used for macramé jewelry are shown below. Most come in a variety of colors and sizes.*

Leather thong

Waxed linen

Three-ply nylon

Metallic twist

Three-ply cotton fleck twine

Two-ply linen

Package twine

#18 waxed nylon

#18 waxed linen

Cotton embroidery floss

Rayon Embroidery floss

Woolen yarn

Wool rug yarn

Jewelry Metals

The metals most commonly used for jewelry are silver, gold, copper, brass, bronze, and pewter. In this book, the emphasis will be on the use of silver, copper, and brass only; gold, bronze, and pewter may be substituted if desired.

There are two types of metal: ferrous (those containing iron or steel) and non-ferrous. The metals covered here all belong to the non-ferrous category. These metals may be purchased in several forms, each of which is suitable for a number of jewelry-making techniques. Available in ingot form for jewelry processes requiring casting, they also come in the form of various thicknesses (gauges) and shapes of sheet and wire. In the United States, the Brown and Sharpe gauge system is used as the standard thickness indicator for sheet and wire. Gauges run from 1 to 40, with a decrease in thickness from .289 inch (1 gauge) to .00314 inch (40 gauge). Gauge size is usually marked on or attached to wire or sheet sold at such commercial outlets as scrap metal businesses, foundries, jewelry supply shops, hardware stores, and hobby shops. Check the Yellow Pages of your phone book under the specific names of the metals, under "jewelry supplies," and under "scrap metals." Also check listings for "hobby supply centers." If there are no local outlets in your area, other sources are available from which metal can be ordered; for a partial listing, see page 80. Be sure to indicate length, width or diameter, and thickness when ordering sheet or wire.

Silver. A soft, malleable metal, silver is the whitest of all metals. The purer the silver, the whiter and softer it becomes. Since pure silver is too soft for most jewelry making, it is alloyed with other metals to add strength; copper is the alloy most commonly used. When 925 parts of silver are combined with 75 parts of copper, sterling silver is produced. Sterling silver sheet and wire have been used extensively in this book where metal jewelry is discussed. Using silver adds a very special feeling of quality and permanence to handcrafted work.

Gold. Like fine silver, pure gold is too soft for use in most jewelry work and is mixed with various alloys to add strength, reduce cost and control color. Measured in karats (K), pure gold is placed as 24K. From 24K to 10K, gold can legally be marked with the karat stamp; below 10K the percentage of alloy outweighs the gold. The number of the karat indicates how many parts out of 24 are gold; for example, 14 karat gold has 14 parts gold to 10 parts alloy. For jewelry, gold is most often used in the forms of 14K and 18K.

When purchasing gold in sheet and wire forms, remember that gold is much heavier than silver; an 18-gauge sheet of gold will outweigh an 18-gauge sheet of silver by almost two to one. Not only will your project weigh more but also its cost for raw materials will be considerably more. Gold is extremely expensive and should be used only when you feel confident in your ability to avoid costly mistakes.

Copper. A relatively soft, malleable, reddish-colored metal that has a tendency to oxidize quickly unless mixed with one of a number of other metals, copper is used extensively in metal enameling. It is the most inexpensive and most easily purchased of the metals mentioned here. Most hardware and craft stores carry copper wire and copper foil for tooling. Copper sheet is most likely to be found at scrap metal outlets.

Brass. A mixture of copper and zinc, brass is a bright yellow-toned metal. It has been used extensively for jewelry in many African and Middle Eastern countries. Brass is also sold in both sheet and wire forms, usually by the same sources recommended for locating copper.

Bronze. By alloying copper with another metal — in this case, tin — bronze is formed. This mixture produces a yellowish red-brown metal that can vary from quite soft to steel hard, depending on the variation in the proportions of copper mixed with tin.

Pewter. When copper is mixed with both antimony and tin, pewter is produced, a metal once widely used in the production of inexpensive table service and plate. Quite soft, pewter is not very often suitable for jewelry requiring fine workmanship or great strength because it is easily scratched or bent out of shape. Both bronze and pewter sheet or wire are available from the suppliers listed on page 80.

Leather: Hide and Thong

Made from the tanned and treated skins of various kinds of animals, leather is a flexible, porous material. Because of its smooth surface and strength, it is a good material for jewelry-making.

Tanned leather can be treated in a number of ways to produce a variety of surface, flex, and color characteristics. One of the most commonly produced types is latigo leather, a cowhide tanned with animal oils. The oils impart a soft, slightly oily surface to the leather, as well as a useful flexibility. Latigo is most often sold in shades of brown, red, black, or yellow. The yellow shade of latigo is easily dyed or painted, providing a background for a number of special treatments used to good effect in making jewelry. Its most common thicknesses range from 3/16 inch (12 ounces) to 1/64 inch (1 ounce). (Thickness is measured by the weight in ounces of one square foot of the leather in question.) Because leather is often sold in scrap form, beads, belt strips, dangles, chokers, and any number of other elements can be effectively and inexpensively produced from scrap leather.

Leather can also be cut into thongs. A large, flat piece of leather is cut into a circle; then a special tool is used to cut a continuous spiral of leather in a specific width. These thongs can be used for braiding, plaiting, macramé, or stringing beads (if thin enough). For local leather sources, check the Yellow Pages of your phone book under the listings for "leather supplies."

Odds and Ends

Almost everyone is a collector of sorts. You may have on hand some pebbles or colorful stones picked up while hiking, or perhaps a few exceptionally nice shells combed from the beaches of some vacation island. Old coins, buttons, beads, bits and pieces of broken but still interesting mechanical oddities all turn up at some time or other in drawers or little jars around the house. If you have other favorite odds and ends or mementos you'd like to keep out for the world to see, what about using them in your handmade jewelry? Many of the projects in this book include found objects as a part of their

Jewelry odds and ends *(clockwise from lower right): striped telephone wire, pheasant feather pelt, drilled seashell, fruit pit beads, tusk shells and coral, sand dollar, shark tooth, brass swivel, brass washers and screws, seashell, feathers by the inch, glass snake beads, coral bead strand, aventurine bead strand, magnolia seed pod, Caribbean seashell, foreign coins, novelty figurines, bone cross-section, and, underneath it all, glossy print magazine pages for paper beads.*

basic materials. A few examples may be seen on pages 36, 45, and 68, and on the preceding page.

Included in this realm of found objects are small items adapted from their originally intended uses to some new applications. Many interesting bits and pieces can be found in hardware stores, hobby shops, plastics supply houses, dime stores, and sewing centers. Following are suggestions for displaying odds and ends featured in several of the jewelry projects in this book.

Coins brought back from visits to foreign countries can be included in your jewelry. Drill one or two holes through the coin and add it to your project. You may legally cut out images from American coins and use the images in your jewelry as long as they aren't mutilated or altered. If you'd like to wear a special coin (say an old twenty dollar gold piece), purchase coin holders from a jewelry supply source and mount the coin in the holder before attaching it to your project.

Feathers add delicacy and airiness to your jewelry pieces. They can be domestic or exotic in origin and are sold in a rainbow of colors. Hobby stores and craft shops often supply small packets of dyed feathers regularly used for feather flower arrangements. Adapt these to your own needs. Natural undyed feathers are supplied by specialty craft shops and can also be found in packet form at sports centers specializing in materials used to tie flies for trout fishing. Feathers are also sold in pelts. An entire birdskin can be purchased and the feathers pulled from the pelt as needed. These feathers must be cleaned and trimmed along the shaft with a single-edge razor blade before they can be used. Scrape off any fuzz and trim the shaft to the necessary length before adding the feather to your jewelry. Feathers are often used in macrame and can also be glued to a leather backing for a solidly feathered appearance. For the best appearance, remember to overlap the feathers as you glue them down.

To make *fruit pit beads* from the pits of peaches, plums, apricots, or nectarines, save the pits when you've eaten the fruit. After you dry them out on the window sill, sand them down and polish their surfaces. Drill a hole through each pit and string them for a novel effect.

Hardware stores are almost inexhaustible sources for supplies. They provide such trinkets as *brass washers* and *wood screws.* Washers can be strung on necklaces or bracelets, used for earrings, or sewn onto leather for an African look. Wood screws become forceful fake studs in metal or wood. *Binder rings,* used for holding punched loose-leaf writing paper, can lead a double life as key rings; *barrel swivels,* small brass attachments used to join hooks and sinkers to fishing line, can be transformed into links or made into chains. Swivels are sold in a number of sizes, making a great variety of appearances possible. For an idea of how swivels can be used, note the key chain shown on page 69.

Don't overlook *magazines and books* as good sources for jewelry materials. Smooth-surfaced, glossy printed pages can serve to make paper beads (see page 25) or be cut up into small bits and made into miniature collages. Just add a pin back and you can wear your creation. Useful, too, are old-fashioned package stickers and greeting cards.

Seeds and shells are two other found objects that can make unusual jewelry. Seeds and seed pods can be dried, pierced, and then strung with beads. Shells, with their unusual shapes and subtle colors, can add natural beauty to anything you might make. To attach shells to your work, either drill holes in each shell or glue bell caps (see "Jewelry Findings," page 6) onto each shell to facilitate stringing them.

Semiprecious stones or *beads* make a handsome focal point for your handmade jewelry pieces. Jewelry supply stores and catalogues usually offer a large selection of stones in various colors and sizes. Semiprecious beads are often carried by import stores, antique shops, and better craft and bead supply stores.

Don't overlook the possibility of adapting various kinds of *wires* for use in your jewelry. Wire is one of the more versatile products carried by hardware, automotive, and electrical supply stores. It comes covered with colored plastic or wrapped with insulating materials; it can be hollow, solid, thick, thin, and made in a variety of colors. If you can locate a source for it, telephone box wire provides a marvelous raw material for jewelry. This is very fine wire covered with plastic in bright, lively colors, often applied in stripes.

Woods and Related Materials

Wood, cardboard, and utility wood products can be used to create unusual jewelry forms. Here are a few suggestions for the use of wood and wood-related materials.

Hardwoods and softwoods. Lightweight, satiny-finished jewelry can be constructed from woods, using only a handsaw, sandpaper, a pocket knife, and perhaps a drill.

Woods can be divided into two groups: hardwoods and softwoods. Because of their unusual colors and grain patterns and their response to careful crafting, hardwoods, rather than softwoods, are used for jewelry. Lumber supply yards sometimes carry common hardwoods like walnut; otherwise you will have to locate a source. In larger cities one or two lumberyards may offer a selection of hardwoods. If they don't have what you need, they may be able to order it or give you the name of a nationally known supplier. Some of the suppliers listed on page 80 offer exotic woods. Although softwoods may be used for jewelry, they don't always finish up as smoothly as hardwoods, nor is the selection of color very broad.

Exotic hardwoods are also available in the form of veneers. These thin pieces of wood can be bent into pleasing shapes or stacked and glued to form a sort of hardwood plywood. When stacking, be sure to alternate the grain direction of each layer of veneer.

Wood derivatives. This group of materials includes such diverse items as cardboard, paper, and manufactured wood products such as toothpicks and lollipop sticks, wooden dowels, and molding. These can all be used to make jewelry.

Cardboard can be glued together and painted, used as a backing for collages, or glued, stacked, and carved into three-dimensional shapes.

Toothpicks adapt easily to being inlaid in wood (see page 48), being colored and then overlaid in a pattern on a plain wood surface, or being built and trimmed into a sculptural form with glue and a pocket knife. The same is true of lollipop sticks.

Wooden dowels and moldings can be cut up into beads, glued together and sliced into sections, or even cut up and collaged onto a flat surface.

Natural and Artificial Finishes

Most jewelry projects should have a finish of some sort applied before they can be considered truly completed. Here's a list of finishes, their uses, and how to apply them.

Acrylic paint. Sold in art supply and stationery stores, acrylic paint is an easily applied finish. It is composed of finely ground particles of colored plastic suspended in a water base. Acrylic paint goes on smoothly, dries rapidly, and leaves a finish that is water and stain repellent. These paints are easily washed from brushes with warm, soapy water.

Fabric dye. A finish of sorts, fabric dye in its powdered form can be blended with homemade or plastic clays to add color. If you intend to mix powdered dye with clay, wear rubber gloves to keep from dyeing your hands. In its liquid state, fabric dye can be painted over the dried surface of clay, wood, paper, or any other absorbent material to produce a transparent colored finish. Brushes may be rinsed out with warm water.

Nail polish. Provide an easily available and relatively inexpensive plastic coating for small jewelry projects with clear nail polish. Either use the accompanying brush to apply the polish or pour the polish out into a deep glass cup and dip the items to be covered. It will take at least 24 hours for the polish to dry completely, so avoid touching the coated items until they are quite dry. Remember that nail polish does have a tendency to go yellow after a period of time.

Plastic (polyurethane) spray. A vapor-suspended plastic in liquid form, this product is sold in aerosol cans. If a very thin film of plastic is desired, use this spray to coat the surfaces of your project. The dried finish, often used to keep metal from tarnishing or otherwise discoloring, is waterproof, stainproof, and relatively non-yellowing.

Polyurethane varnish. A liquid synthetic varnish resin used to give a clear, glossy finish to almost any kind of material, polyurethane is impervious to water, alcohol, stains of any kind, and most solvents.

Shellac. This is a spirit varnish made from a natural resin. Used almost exclusively on wood, shellac dries to a glossy finish in half an hour. Unfortunately, it is highly susceptible to moisture and a number of solvents, but when used as an undercoat, shellac is quite satisfactory. Clean shellac from brushes with shellac thinner.

Shoe polish. Use shoe polish to stain and give a waxy finish to wood, leather, or clay. Clear or natural polish is often applied to finish leather. This type of finish must be renewed occasionally because it will gradually wear off.

Varnish. Put to the same use as shellac, varnish is much more durable. Usually made from synthetic resins, varnish resists stains from water or other liquids and from a number of solvents. One drawback of varnish, though, is its slow drying time. It takes several hours before a varnished surface loses its tackiness and sets up a hard finish. Varnish remover will effectively clean varnish-laden brushes.

Wood lacquer. Originally made from the sap of certain trees, wood lacquer is cured to make a hard, durable, waterproof finish. Now most lacquers are made from synthetic materials. Lacquer produces a finish about equal to varnish in durability but with a much shinier surface quality. To clean lacquer from your brushes, use lacquer thinner.

Wood oils. Sold in paint supply stores, these oils bring out and intensify the natural color of woods. The oil is rubbed on with a soft cloth and left for half an hour; then any excess is removed with a clean, soft cloth. This is repeated several times until the wood has absorbed all the oil it can. Oil will help to protect against water stains, but only if spilled water is wiped up quickly. An inexpensive and readily available substitute is mineral oil. For extra protection, wax over the oil finish with a good furniture wax.

Wood sealers. Apply this finish to seal the surfaces of previously untreated woods. It is a clear penetrating liquid that can be wiped on with a soft rag, left to set for half an hour, and then removed with another soft rag. Wood sealer is a transparent finish that leaves the sealed wood similar in appearance to its condition before being sealed. Soak brushes in paint thinner to clean them.

Wood wax. Give a final protective coating to various wood finishes by applying wood wax. Used by itself, though, wax is not particularly effective at protecting a wood surface against anything but water stains.

Some Helpful Tools

The tools and equipment used to construct jewelry can range from specially made precision pieces to general carpentry tools. Some equipment can be constructed rather than bought; it's also sometimes possible to substitute carpentry and automotive tools for those pieces of equipment made only to be used for articles of jewelry. Such substitutions, where possible, are discussed under each of the following headings. If no substitution can be made, use the information given on page 80 to locate catalogue sources for jewelry equipment, unless, of course, there is a jewelry supply store in your area. To find out, check the Yellow Pages of your phone book under "jewelry supplies."

Bench Tools

This group of tools includes those most essential for the making of the majority of jewelry projects covered in this book. Although there will be other tools under other headings that may be considered important, these are the basics.

Anvil. Also called a beck-iron, the anvil is used as a base on which metal pieces are hammered and shaped through the use of a hammer or mallet. You can purchase an anvil from a jewelry supply source, or you can make one of your own by using the face of a discarded clothes iron or a steel I-beam (a slice cut from a building girder). For ideas, see the photograph on page 13.

Bench pins. Defined as wedge-shaped pieces of wood, sometimes having a V-shaped opening cut in the narrow end of the wedge, bench pins are used as supports for drilling, sawing, cutting, filing, or other close work. The pin is either clamped to the edge of the working surface or attached directly to the edge of the work table with screws. A bench pin can be cut and shaped from a standard 2 x 4. This is one piece of equipment that need not be purchased ready-made. Bench pins are shown in the photograph on the facing page.

Butane torch. An inexpensive butane torch with accessories (available in hardware stores) is useful for working with metals of any kind. As metals are bent, hammered, or reshaped in any way, they become stiff and brittle. To prevent cracks or outright breakage, the stiffened metal is *annealed* before forming is continued. Annealing consists of heating the metal until it takes on a dull red glow and then quenching it by dunking it quickly into a pail of cold water. The heat expands the molecules in the metal and the quick dunking in cold water "freezes" the molecules in their expanded condition.

C-clamps. Various sizes of C-clamps are handy tools for the jewelry workbench. Used in conjunction with bench pins, wood blocks, glue setting, and any number of purposes, C-clamps are easily and inexpensively purchased from any hardware store.

Drills and bits. Put to many uses when making jewelry, drills and bits bore holes for jump rings, for starting jeweler's saws, for making cylindrical inlays in wood or metal, and for decorative effects. Hand drills, electrical drills, or even drill presses can be used for jewelry. Hand drills are the most versatile and, in most cases,

the most suitable, especially when you're working with delicate materials. Pressure and speed are more easily controlled with a hand drill. On the other hand, when many holes must be drilled or a material is particularly dense or hard, the electric drill is more useful. When drilling accuracy is essential, presses work best. The types of drills and drill bits that can be used for jewelry are shown in the photographs on page 13.

Drill bits are sized by diameter in the larger bits and by a numbered progression in smaller sizes. The largest drill bits can measure up to 1 inch in diameter; the smallest (#80) is less than half the thickness of a common straight pin. Go slowly and use only light pressure while drilling with a very small bit; small bits bend and break quite easily.

Hammers. These can range from specialty tools available through jewelry supply sources, to carpentry hammers. A variety of hammers is used for jewelry; two of the most common are the ball peen hammer, which has one flat end and one round end, and the French chasing hammer, which has one very large flat end and one very small round end. Ball peen hammers are most commonly used for forging sheet and wire, for removing dents from metal surfaces, and for hammering impressions into metal sheet. French chasing hammers are best suited for flattening bent objects, for driving chasing or repoussé tools, and for setting metal rivets.

Small (8 to 12-ounce) carpentry hammers may be substituted for these specialty hammers and will work quite nicely if used carefully. For examples, see the photograph on the facing page.

Jewelry pliers. Available in a wide variety of sizes, shapes, types, and prices, jewelry pliers are precision instruments used to shape and bend both wire and sheet metal. Most jewelry can be worked with just three basic plier types: chainnose pliers have tapered pointed jaws that are half-rounds in shape. These pliers are used to form bends and loops in metal and to grip, pull, or form metals in various jewelry processes.

Flatnose pliers have flat, wedge-shaped jaws for gripping or holding objects with flat surfaces. The jaws are useful for making angular bends.

Roundnose pliers are the most commonly used pliers. Their jaws are tapered, pointed, and cylindrically shaped, well suited for making bends, coils, loops, and circles in sheet or wire metal.

All of these pliers are available through jewelry supply sources and are sometimes carried by hobby and craft centers or even by hardware stores. As substitutes, shop or automotive pliers (sold in hardware and auto supply stores) can be used instead, but first cover the serrated jaws with plastic electrical tape to avoid scarring the metal you are bending. Examples of pliers for jewelry are shown at lower left in the photograph on the facing page.

Screwdrivers. A set of screwdrivers in graduated sizes (either specially made jewelry tools or small-scale automotive tools) is a good investment. Each can be used for purposes other than just setting screws.

Vises. Varying from small, bench-type equipment to a hand-held model, the vise is used to clamp and hold materials while they are being worked on, especially if the craftsman needs to have both hands free. Most useful is the bench vise, which may be temporarily clamped to the work bench or affixed permanently to the table

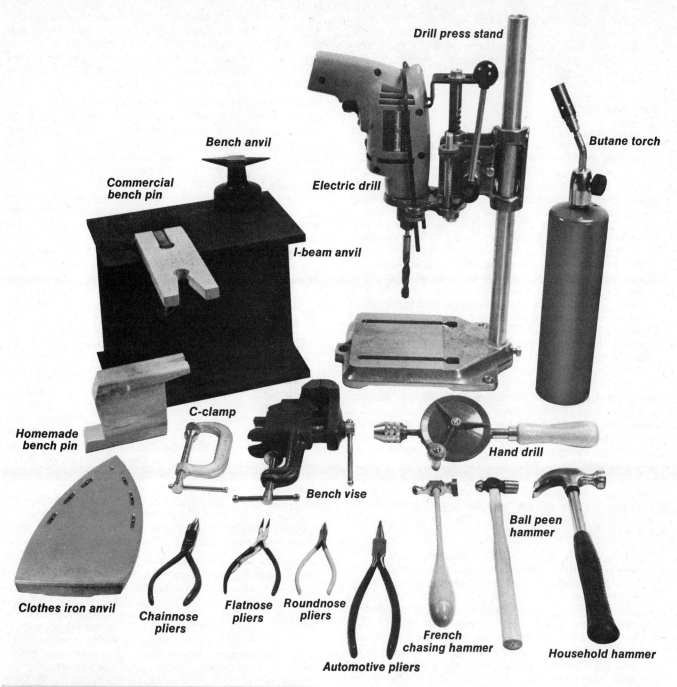

Drill press stand

Bench anvil

Commercial bench pin

Butane torch

Electric drill

I-beam anvil

Homemade bench pin

C-clamp

Hand drill

Bench vise

Ball peen hammer

Clothes iron anvil

Chainnose pliers

Flatnose pliers

Roundnose pliers

French chasing hammer

Household hammer

Automotive pliers

From largest to smallest: *the ½-inch drill bit on the left is probably the largest size used for making jewelry; the tiny #80 drill bit on the right, used for fine jewelry work, is magnified to one and one-half times its normal size.*

JEWELRY TOOLS **13**

with screws. Before using the vise for jewelry work, cover the jaws with soft leather pieces glued into place. Small bench vises are sold in hardware and some hobby supply shops. A bench vise is included in the photograph shown on page 13.

Saw and Blades

If you're planning to make jewelry from metal sheet or exotic woods, a saw is a very important piece of equipment. The blades and handles of saws used for jewelry making are much smaller than those used for other types of cutting jobs. A photograph showing some examples appears on the facing page. Here are some of the saws and blades most commonly used for making jewelry:

Jeweler's saw. The jeweler's saw is similar in appearance to the scroll saw, described below, but its framework is more streamlined and has an adjustable key at the top of its metal frame to make small changes in frame length or blade tension. Used in conjunction with a bench pin (see page 12), this saw is held in a vertical position only, keeping its body *always* at right angles to the surface being cut. Very light pressure is necessary to drive the saw on the downward cutting stroke; its momentum and weight will do the work.

The jeweler's saw utilizes very fine blades, ranging from .0063 inch in width (8/0) to .0236 inch in width (#14), the smaller blades having correspondingly finer toothed cutting edges. For the jewelry projects in this book, blades between 2/0 and #4 are recommended. Jeweler's saw blades come in three categories: piercing (for fine work), flat (for more coarse cuts), and spiral (for rubber and plastics).

Jeweler's saws and blades are carried by hobby and craft supply houses and by some hardware stores. If you aren't able to locate any sources in your area, turn to page 80 of this book for the addresses of the jewelry equipment suppliers listed.

Scroll saw. This is a hand saw frequently used in carpentry for cutting curves and ornamental scrollwork. Simple in appearance, the scroll saw is essentially an arching metal frame (somewhat like a horizontally stretched capital U in appearance) attached to a straight wooden handle. At the point where the handle is attached to one end of the metal arch, there is a thumbscrew and clamp in which one end of an interchangeable saw blade is secured. The other end of the blade is clamped under tension into a similar thumbscrew and clamp at the other end of the metal arch. Though there are special blades made only for the scroll saw, it will also take jeweler's saw blades.

Mounting jeweler's saw blades. To attach a blade to either a scroll or jeweler's saw, first loosen the thumbscrew and clamp at each end of the saw frame. Face the cutting edge of the blade *away* from the saw frame, making sure that the saw teeth point *toward* the saw handle. Then push the end of the saw blade into the open clamp at the unattached end of the saw frame and tighten the key until the blade is secure. Next, place the end of the saw against the edge of your work bench, allowing the frame to hang downward, and brace the handle against your chest. Loosen the key and clamp closest to you; then press against the handle with your chest to compress the metal saw frame. This will allow

the free end of the blade to enter the open clamp. After tightening the clamp securely, gradually release the pressure on the compressed frame. If you release too quickly, the blade will snap. When properly held in the frame, the blade should be absolutely taut and give off a high-pitched "ping" when plucked.

Using fine-bladed saws. Small saw blades have a tendency to be brittle and are easily broken. To use them properly, follow these suggestions: 1) Don't force the blade or use pressure of any sort; the blades break easily under pressure. To keep the blade working smoothly, lubricate it with beeswax. 2) Work slowly to avoid losing control of the blade. 3) To cut around sharp angles or abrupt turns in a design, saw up to the turning point; then saw up and down at that point without moving the blade forward. As you saw, gradually turn the whole saw until the teeth are pointed in the direction you wish to go. 4) When starting a cut within an enclosed area, first drill a hole within the area to be cut out. Then thread one end of the sawblade down through the hole and refasten it to the saw. When you've finished cutting, loosen the blade and remove it in the same manner. 5) As you saw, cut on the waste side of the design outline. If you make any mistakes in cutting, it's easier to repair them when you can sand or file back to the design outline.

Jigsaw. To make preliminary or rough cuts in wood or plastic that is up to 1¾ inch thick or in a metal sheet that is 18 gauge or thicker, use a jigsaw. As opposed to hand saws where the saw and blade are mobile, the jigsaw blade is driven up and down by a motor and is housed in a large stationary assembly. Since this saw can remain stationary while the material being cut is guided into the blade by hand, cutting is faster and, in many cases, easier than with a handsaw.

Jigsaws can cut very intricate designs very rapidly, but controlling this fast cutting action takes practice. It's usually safer to make precision cuts or to do fine work more slowly by hand with a jeweler's or scroll saw.

Miter box saw and miter box. To cut accurate 45° and 90° angles for joining corners or for lamination work, a miter box and saw are essential. The box itself has accurately pre-cut channels made at 45° and 90° angles in the box. The materials to be cut are marked and then slid into the miter box to be lined up with the proper cutting channel. The saw blade — rectangular in shape with fine teeth on one of its longer edges — is placed in the desired set of channels, which guides the movement of the blade as it cuts. Then the cut is made while the material is held under pressure.

Saber saw. The saber saw, also called a portable jigsaw, is a lightweight power tool with interchangeable blades. It's used primarily to break down large pieces of wood, plastic, or metal sheet into workable sizes. Since the saw cuts rapidly and leaves an unfinished cut edge, it is best suited for preliminary work and rough cutting.

Files, Abrasives, and Buffing Tools

No matter how much time is spent on shaping, sawing, or otherwise working a piece of jewelry, any rough edges or dull, scratched surfaces will detract from the beauty of even the most clever design. Your piece won't be completed until you've filed, sanded, buffed, and polished it to a smooth finish. When jewelry is handled, it should

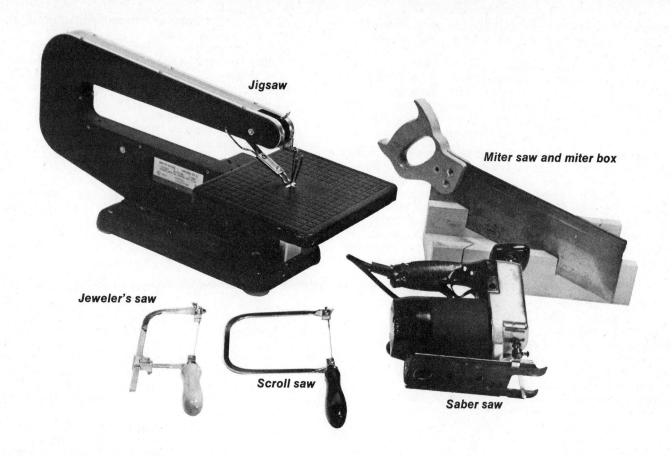

Jigsaw

Miter saw and miter box

Jeweler's saw

Scroll saw

Saber saw

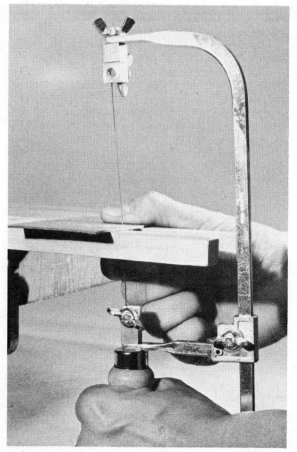

The jeweler's saw *should always be used in an upright position, as shown in the photograph at left. No force is needed to drive the blade other than the weight of the jeweler's saw itself.*

Brace the saw frame *between the bench edge and your chest to mount a saw blade (see facing page), putting pressure on the frame as the blade is inserted into the clamp.*

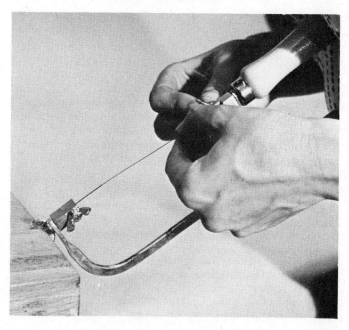

have the feel of quality that a good finish suggests; the work and time you've put into the piece call for nothing less.

Remember that any filing or polishing is done *before* the separate parts of a piece of jewelry are joined together. Don't mount jump rings, semi-precious stones, or other fragile parts until you've completed *all* polishing steps. The following paragraphs tell you how to achieve a good finish for your handmade jewelry.

Files and how to use them. Hand files come in two sizes and in a variety of shapes. For rough finishing to remove excess metal, wood, or plastic, use round, half-round, or flat #4 mill smooth files. For finer surface finishing, work with needle or rattail files. These are small, fine-toothed files, each about 5½ inches in length. They come in a wide range of shapes, the most common of which are the equaling (rectangular), half-round, knife (triangular), square, and round files (examples are shown on the facing page). These can be found in some hardware stores, hobby and craft shops, or jewelry supply outlets. To locate a catalogue source for them, see the list of suppliers on page 80.

Files aren't difficult to use; just remember to work diagonally across the surface being filed and to change directions frequently to avoid scarring. Work the file itself in one direction only, from the tip of the file to the handle, and use medium to light pressure. The material being filed should be held in a clamp or vise to keep it steady; otherwise hold the piece on the surface of the bench pin as you file.

To keep files in good working condition, clean them periodically to remove metal filings. Special brushes are available for cleaning files; or use a stiff-bristled toothbrush and detergent, then rinse off the files, dry them thoroughly, and coat them with machine oil to prevent rust from forming.

Abrasive coated papers and cloths. To remove file marks, pits, or scratches, work with abrasive papers and cloths. These are sheets of heavy-duty paper or stiff cloth covered with particles of emery (corundum), silicon carbide, or garnet. Emery and silicon carbide are used to sand metals and plastics, whereas garnet abrasive works best when used for wood.

Grading in abrasive papers can take two different forms: grit symbols, which run from #4½ (very coarse) to 10/0 (very fine), and mesh numbers, which range from #12 (coarse), to #600 (very fine). Most finishing work is done with medium and fine abrasives.

For easier handling, tear off small pieces of abrasive paper or cloth and fold them into shapes that adapt to the surfaces being sanded. Moisten the emery or silicon carbide papers for extra cutting power. To produce a well-sanded surface, use medium pressure and develop a rhythm in your arm movements as you work.

Buffing by hand or by machine. Remove tool and sanding marks by buffing. This finishing process makes use of a cloth or brush charged with polishing compound. The cloth or brush is worked over filed and sanded surfaces to polish out any scratches or dull areas. Buffing can be done by hand or by machine.

Used in conjunction with both hand and motor-driven buffs, tripoli and rouge compounds are composed of grits or powders mixed with wax to a heavy, pastelike consistency that is compressed into bars or packed into tins. When applied with stick or wheel buffs, these compounds bring out the shine and smooth surface qualities inherent in metal and plastic.

Tripoli (a silica powder compound) is the first buffing compound to be used. It is more coarse than rouge and has more cutting power. Rouge (red iron oxide), which comes in different colors for use with different metals, is the final buffing compound. It is used to bring out the luster of the polished surface.

When buffing is done by hand, a soft cloth or a wooden stick covered with felt or leather is charged with tripoli and rubbed with medium pressure across the area to be polished. When this stage of buffing is finished, the tripoli is rinsed off the project and another buff is loaded with rouge. (Be sure to use separate buffs for the tripoli and for the rouge.) This second buffing will bring the piece to a high state of polish.

Buffing goes more quickly when an electrically powered wheel is used. Special motors and housings are available from jewelry and hardware supply outlets. These mounted and shielded motors drive rotating shafts to which wheel-shaped buffs can be attached. After tripoli or rouge is applied to the rims of these spinning buffs, the jewelry piece is held against the charged rim and moved about until polished to your satisfaction. The motor-powered buffing wheel gives a very good polished finish. The buffs themselves range from stacked layers of cotton fabric circles stitched together to stiff boar bristle brushes or thick felt pads. A photograph showing a selection of hand and machine buffs can be seen on the facing page.

To achieve at a lower cost the same effect the electric buffing wheel gives, purchase buffing wheel attachments for your power hand drill. Mount the buffs onto the drill and lock the drill handle tightly in the jaws of a bench vise. The drill can now be used as a makeshift electrical buffing wheel.

For safety, remember to wear protective goggles *at all times* when using electric wheels; they will protect your eyes from flying pieces of metal or buffing compound. To protect your hands while working on a motor-driven buff, hold the jewelry piece properly against the wheel. The correct position for buffing is shown in the photograph at lower left on the facing page. To polish wire jewelry or other pieces of fragile construction, support them with a piece of scrap wood as shown in the photograph mentioned above. As you work, keep the piece in motion and don't apply too much pressure; the force of the spinning buff will be quite adequate for removing scratches.

The final polish. This step should be done only by hand. Remove any abrasives still on the jewelry piece; then use an old, soft-bristled toothbrush, hot water, and detergent to clean it. After you dry the piece with tissue or a soft cloth, go over all surfaces with a felt buff stick charged with rouge. When you've finished polishing, clean off the rouge and rub the piece with a soft cloth. For a matte finish, give the piece a final polish with #00 steel wool, rubbing in one direction only. This will leave the polished surface with a soft, brushed appearance.

Measuring Tools

To make accurate measurements of materials and to mark guidelines at the right places as you work, keep these tools handy: a compass, a 6-inch ruler, a tape measure,

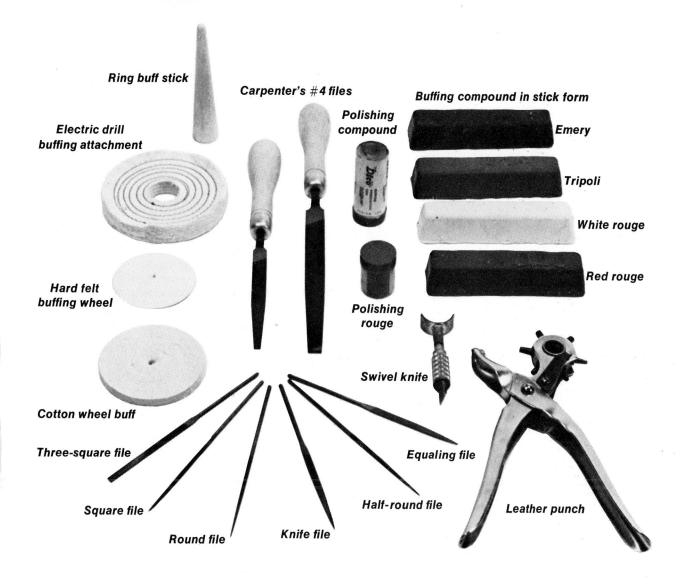

Ring buff stick

Electric drill buffing attachment

Carpenter's #4 files

Polishing compound

Buffing compound in stick form

Emery

Tripoli

White rouge

Hard felt buffing wheel

Red rouge

Polishing rouge

Cotton wheel buff

Swivel knife

Three-square file

Equaling file

Square file

Half-round file

Leather punch

Round file

Knife file

The proper position *in which to hold jewelry while buffing is shown at left. Light pressure against the wheel is all that's needed to give a good polish. Delicate pieces and chains are protected by holding or wrapping them against a piece of thin scrap plywood before buffing as shown in the photograph.*

and a yardstick. The compass and short ruler are most often used when working with metal, wood, plastic, or other hard materials. When fibers are used, a tape measure and a yardstick can come in handy for measuring off long lengths of yarn or cord.

Cutting Tools

Because different jewelry materials have different characteristics, a variety of tools is needed to cut them. Clay, leather, and wood are best cut with blades. This category includes razor blades, art knives, pocket knives, and blunt table knives. Paper, cloth, yarn, cord, and thin metal sheet can be cut with scissors. Household scissors, embroidery scissors, and manicure scissors do progressively finer cutting jobs. Metal sheet and very thick leather respond to the powerful jaws of a metal snip, a scissorslike tool with heavy beak-shaped jaws; metal wire, on the other hand, can be cut with electrical wire cutters. Snips and wire cutters are sold in hardware stores.

Needles and Pins

Blunt-nosed tapestry needles can do more than just sew. Use them for making paper beads (see page 25), for piercing clay beads, for tooling thin copper sheet (see page 55), and for finishing wrapped yarn projects. Glass-headed or T-pins are used for macramé projects to hold down knotted areas while they are being worked on.

Cements and Glues

Sometimes it is necessary to bond two or more surfaces together when working on jewelry. Glues are used for bonding findings to the backs of jewelry pieces, laminating hardwoods together, joining different materials, holding fibers in place, and for hundreds of other purposes. Different materials and purposes call for different kinds of glues or cements; here are some of the bonding compounds available at most hardware or craft stores:

Epoxy cement, an extremely strong, two-part cement, can best be used where a tough permanent bond is required. Mixed from two separate tubes, one containing resin, the other, hardener, epoxy is most useful for applying findings to finished jewelry pieces, bonding metal and wood, or joining almost any material at points of stress. Curing time for epoxy ranges from a bare 5 minutes to over 48 hours.

Plastic transparent glues are used for hobby work and general household repairs. Clear-drying but somewhat brittle, these adhesives work well on any material where an invisible bond is desired.

Rubber cement should be used where a temporary or semipermanent join is necessary. This adhesive is sold in a glue-pot-shaped bottle equipped with a brush. A thin layer of cement is brushed over both surfaces to be bonded and allowed to become tacky; then the surfaces are pressed together. This forms a semipermanent bond on papers, cardboard, leather, and some plastics. For a more temporary bond, apply cement to only one of the surfaces and bond the surfaces while the cement is still wet. Rubber cement can be removed with a special pick-up eraser and rubber cement solvent.

White glues are milk-colored, polyvinyl resin adhesives that have many uses. Sold in large squeeze bottles, this glue gives a medium-strength, clear-drying bond to a wide range of materials.

Resorcinol resin glue is a two-part adhesive ideally suited to bonding woods together when strength and resistance to water are necessary. This glue has a curing time of about 12 hours; the pieces being glued should be clamped while the glue is drying.

Brushes

When a piece of jewelry requires painting or gluing, brushes will come in handy. Some surfaces, such as leather, paper, and wood, can be decorated by painting designs on their surfaces or by coloring them with dyes. Use a fine camel's hair brush (a #00 is a good size) for this purpose. To apply the correct amount of glue to a specific area of a jewelry piece, use a small, stiff-bristled brush and clean it with solvent after each glue application. Most art supply or stationery stores will carry a selection of brushes to choose from.

Miscellaneous Equipment

Following is a list of odds and ends of equipment you may find helpful when constructing your jewelry:

Carbon paper, sold by stationery supply stores, is used to transfer designs from tracing paper to the surface of your jewelry material. Tape it to the surface of the material, place the design over it, then re-trace slowly over the design with a ballpoint pen.

Ceiling tile (Celotex) is a soft, fibrous board with a white-painted surface. It is used extensively for macramé work. The piece being knotted is anchored to this board with glass-headed or T-pins and further secured to the board as work on the macramé piece progresses. Ceiling tile is sold in lumber supply and some craft stores.

Graph paper is useful for scaling designs up or down in size and for indicating intricate pattern work in macramé (see page 23). Sold in stationery supply stores, graph paper comes in a wide range of grid sizes, the most useful of which is the 10-squares-to-the-inch size.

A *leather punch* makes belt notches, holes for key rings, decorative leather punching, and can also be used for punching holes in thin sheet metal. Punches usually consist of a wheel of interchangeable punch tips in graduating sizes attached to a pair of long handles (a leather punch is shown on page 17).

Scribing tools can be made from anything with a strong, semisharp point, such as a ballpoint pen, a toothpick, or various tapestry needles. Scribing consists of scoring marks into the surface of jewelry material to place a pattern or design that will be finished by cutting, filing, or painting.

Tracing paper is sold in stationery stores in tablets of varying sheet size. Use tracing paper to work out your jewelry designs and patterns; then glue them with rubber cement to the material being cut or tooled, and work with the design in place. Tracing paper can also be used for copying designs from books or magazines.

Wooden dowels can help you to roll out dough, punch holes, and apply glue. You can also clean jewelry pieces with dowels having a cotton puff taped to one end.

A *wool dauber* is a square of sheepskin cut from scrap and used for applying leather dyes. The wool side of the skin holds the dye and acts as a spreader.

Macramé for Jewelry

Whole books have been devoted to the craft of macramé, so this short, one-page section on knot-tying will serve only as a handy guide to the knots and materials used for the macramé jewelry projects in this book.

The cords and yarns best suited for macramé jewelry work are those with tightly plied, smooth surfaces; this quality allows each knot to stand out sharply. For fine work, the smaller the diameter of the cord, the better the detail. Cords and yarns are discussed in more detail on page 6.

When estimating the total lengths of the cords to be used for a piece of macramé jewelry, only a rough cal-culation can be worked out; cord lengths should be about eight to ten times as long as the finished project. Remember: The more knots that you have to tie with a cord, the faster it is used up.

Long lengths of cord are easier to work with when they've been gathered up into a bobbin wrapped with a rubber band. The illustration (below, center) shows how to make a bobbin. The knots shown below represent only about half of the knots used for projects in this book; the remaining knots are illustrated on the same pages as the projects in which they are used. These projects are located on pages 22, 26, 39, 40, and 42.

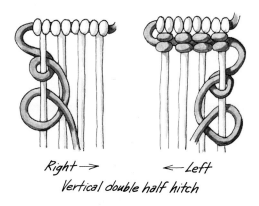

Right →   ← Left

Vertical double half hitch

Square knot

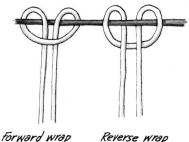

Forward wrap   Reverse wrap

Mounting knots

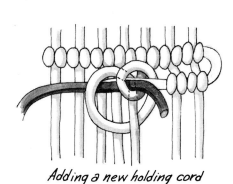

Adding a new holding cord

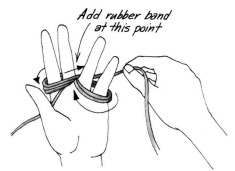

Add rubber band at this point

Making a butterfly cord bobbin

Vertical reverse double half hitch chain

Handcrafted Jewelry

Watch Strap Bracelet
(page 40)

Sea Shells and Silver Necklace
(page 25)

Two-Tone Cufflinks
(page 49)

Smart as Paint Leather Barrettes
(page 35)

Projects

**Chain of Beads Necklace
(page 30)**

Beautiful handmade jewelry isn't beyond your reach; it's no farther away than the next page. From this point on you can sift through more than 40 jewelry designs for anything from a simple tie tack to a spectacular feather and macramé necklace — all made without using expensive and difficult processes. Small amounts of silver sheet and wire will be the most expensive materials you will have to buy.

Complete directions for the techniques required to make each project are accompanied by detailed illustrations showing you exactly how to produce a stunning finished piece. And each piece of jewelry offered as a project is shown in color on one of 16 color pages spread throughout the following chapter.

For more information on some of the tools and materials used in these projects, see pages 6 through 19. From the suppliers listed on page 80, certain materials and equipment that may not be readily available in your area can be ordered.

Oaxaca Choker

(Color photo on page 28)

Even the most sophisticated of tastes will appreciate the native beauty of this handmade macramé choker. Time consuming though not difficult to make, this necklace uses mainly two knots: the horizontal double half hitch and the vertical double half hitch. These knots are combined according to the pattern given on the facing page; transferred to graph paper with 10 squares to the inch, it becomes an accurate chart for the two-color design. The winged pattern decorating the choker bands was inspired by designs from the Zapotec culture found on a structure in Mitla, Oaxaca, Mexico. Find more information on macramé and detailed illustrations of individual knots by turning to page 19.

Equipment: One 12-inch by 12-inch square of composition board, T-pins or glass-headed pins, one sheet of 10-squares-to-the-inch graph paper, ballpoint pen, scissors, yardstick or tape measure.

Materials: 112 yards of old gold #18 waxed nylon cord; 34 yards of hunter green #18 waxed nylon cord; twenty-seven ³⁄₁₆-inch-diameter, topaz-colored beads; white glue.

How to Make

1. To make the right side of the choker, cut four 100-inch lengths of gold cord and pin the four ends together at the very top of the working board. Measure 24 inches down the cords and mark with a pin. At this point, tie a square knot (see page 19), using the two middle cords as holding cords and the two outside cords as working cords.

2. Cut eight 200-inch-long gold cords and fold each in half. Directly below the square knot, begin to add in these 200-inch lengths, one at a time and centered on the square knot as shown in illustration A, gradually increasing the width of the choker band to 1⅛ inch.

3. Cut twelve 100-inch-long green cords and use them as needed (see page 19 for adding on cords). The first cord is started by adding it to the last four horizontal double half hitch knots on the right edge of the

eighth added gold cord (see illustration on page 19).

4. With this secondary color cord as the holding cord, work seven rows of horizontal double half hitch knots, setting the width of the choker band at about 1¼ inch.

5. At this point, transfer the complete design on the facing page to 10-squares-to-the-inch graph paper. Each clear square represents one horizontal double half hitch knot and each dotted square indicates one vertical double half hitch knot. Pin the graph to your working surface, using it to mark off rows and knots as you work, to keep track of the order of the design. Remember, you have already completed eight rows of work.

6. Work rows 9 through 15 in horizontal double half hitch knots.

7. The two-color pattern begins in row 16. Follow the graph for the correct number of each knot to tie. Horizontal double half hitches are *always* tied in gold; vertical double half hitches (see page 19) are *always* tied in green. As an example, work row 16 from left to right, tying 15 *horizontal* double half hitches and using the green cord as the holding cord. Then tie three *vertical* double half hitches with the green cord and use the gold cords as holding cords. Complete the row with two horizontal double half hitches. The row should look like the one in illustration B.

8. Continue the pattern through row 45, following the procedure given in step 7.

9. Rows 46 through 48 are horizontal double half hitches.

10. Continue to follow the graphed pattern from rows 49 through 68. In row 69, leave untied the first two gold cords coming down from row 68 on the left. Work through row 70; then taper off again when starting row 71 by leaving untied the first two gold cords coming down from row 70 on the left. Continue this procedure by tapering off every other row (rows 71, 73, 75, 77, 79, 81, 83, 85) in the same manner (refer to the graph).

11. When row 85 has been completed, you will have nine pairs of dropped gold cords tapering down from left to right, one green holding cord, and two gold tying cords at the very point of the taper.

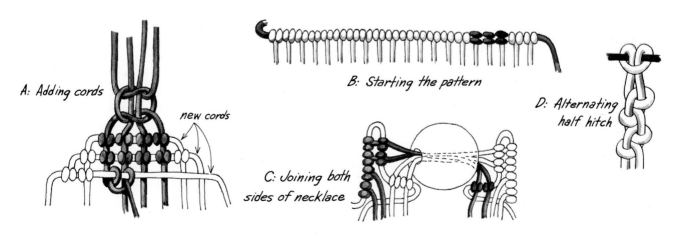

A: Adding cords

new cords

B: Starting the pattern

C: Joining both sides of necklace

D: Alternating half hitch

12. Remove the piece from the board and repeat steps 1 through 11 for the second half of the choker band, but reversing the graphed pattern to make it a mirror image of the pattern in the completed choker band. Also go through the steps and rewrite the directions to read *left* instead of right and *right* instead of left (example: "1. To make the *left* side of the choker . . .").

13. When the two sides of the choker band are completed, pin them onto the working board in a horizontal position with their center points together with just enough space between for one bead.

14. To add the bead, pass the two gold tying cords from the left-hand band through the bead to the right side and pass the corresponding cords from the right-hand band through the same bead to the left side.

15. Starting with dropped cords 1 and 2 (see graph) on the left-hand half of the necklace, tie three vertical reverse double half hitches (see page 19), using cord 2 as the holding cord and cord 1 as the tying cord. Repeat for cords 3 and 4, tying two knots; cords 5 and 6, tying two knots; cords 7 and 8, tying one knot; cords 9 and 10, 11 and 12, 13 and 14, all having only one knot. Repeat for the right half of the choker band. The remaining pairs of cords on both bands will be used as they are.

16. Working both sides of the choker pendant at once, start by using the gold cords coming through the bead to tie two horizontal double half hitch knots over the green holding cords as shown in illustration C.

17. Continue to use the green cord as a holding cord and work downward for six more rows, picking up the dropped gold cords from the choker bands at the *outer* end of every other row you work.

18. The eighth row begins the pattern once again. Use the graph and its mirror image from this point on to work through the order of knots and colors.

19. At the end of row 9, mount the second bead by exchanging the left and the right green holding cords *through* the bead. This procedure will be repeated in rows 17, 25, and 33 to add the remaining beads (it will help to put a mark by these rows on the graph to remind yourself). As you work, continue to pick up dropped cords from the vertical reverse double half hitch chains.

20. Continue to use the graph as a guide for color changes and knot alterations, for completing the picking up of dropped cords and for adding on center beads, until row 33 is completed.

21. Work rows 34 through 60 according to the graph.

22. Starting with row 61, follow the directions in step 10 for tapering off the rows. The last two outside gold cords in rows 60, 62, 64, 66, 68, 70, 72, 74, 76, and 77 on both sides of the pendant will be left free.

23. To finish the lower edges of the pendant, tie a sinnet (or chain) of 20 alternating half hitch knots (see page 19) with each pair of dropped gold cords; the last three cords at the center edge of each side have 18 alternating half hitch knots, using the two gold cords as one cord and the green cord as the other. Finish each length by threading on a bead and tying an overhand knot below the bead. Cut off excess cord and dip the knot in white glue.

24. Tie 60 alternating half hitches (illustration D) in the lengths of cord left at the ends of each choker band. Divide the strands into two pairs and use each pair as one strand. When you are finished, thread a bead onto each length, tie an overhand knot after the bead, clip the cords, and dip each knot in white glue.

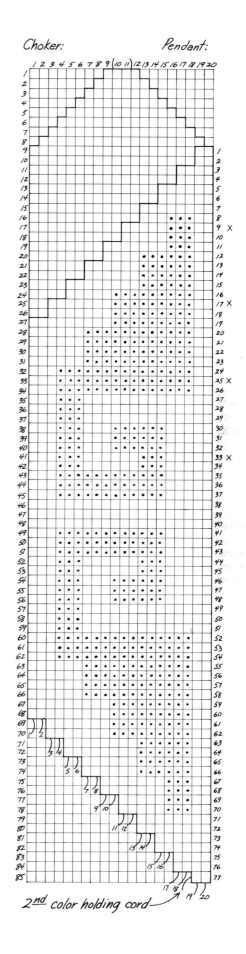

Choker: Pendant:

2nd color holding cord

Trade Bead Necklace

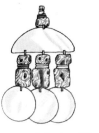

(Color photo on page 28)

This glass trade bead and hammered copper neckpiece could be as old as Africa or as contemporary as today. Thin sheets of copper are cut and hammered into mottled-surfaced tactile discs, which are then strung together with old trade beads onto iron or brass wires. Excitingly primitive in spirit, the metal and bead combinations can be varied to suit your own taste, or you can make your own innovations by redesigning the cut shapes or by adding found objects to the design. The pendant design could also become the basis for a pair of matching earrings. For more information on metals and the tools used, see pages 6-19.

Equipment: Compass, scribing tool, roundnose pliers, metal snips or jeweler's saw and bench pin, household hammer, anvil (see page 12), hand drill, ½-inch drill bit, assorted jeweler's files, tracing paper, scissors.

Materials: 26 inches of 16-gauge dark annealed or soft brass wire, 2½-inch by 4-inch rectangle of 24-gauge sheet brass, three large trade beads, four medium trade beads, one small trade bead, eight clamshell *hishi* beads.

How to Make

1. With a compass, draw a 2-inch-diameter circle on tracing paper and cut it out. Fold the circle in half and use it as a pattern by laying the semicircle on the brass sheet metal and scribing the outline into the metal. With metal snips or jeweler's saw, cut out the semicircle (see cutting pattern below). With a hammer and anvil, forge the metal to give it texture. File off any rough edges.

2. To find the center line of the semicircle, fold the paper pattern in half again and mark the brass where the fold falls. Using the ½-inch drill bit, drill two holes, one at the center top and one at the center bottom of the brass semicircle. Then drill two ½-inch holes, each ½-inch away on *either* side of the hole drilled on the bottom edge of the semicircle. Remove any rough spots with a file.

3. Make a paper pattern for a 1-inch-diameter circle and cut it out. Trace three such circles onto the remaining brass sheet (see below) and cut them out. Drill a ½-inch hole in each metal disc and then file holes and edges to remove rough spots.

4. Cut three pieces of 16-gauge annealed brass wire, each two inches long. Form a small open loop with roundnose pliers at one end of each wire and then thread a metal disc onto each loop. Close loops with pliers.

5. Arrange beads on wires, following photo on page 28. Leaving about ½ inch for loops, snip off excess wire from each length and bend free ends into open loops. Attach them to the lower edge of the semicircle and close loops with pliers.

6. Cut a 2-inch length of 16-gauge brass wire and make an open loop at one end, attaching it to the top of the semicircle. Use pliers to close the loop. Set the metal and bead dangle aside temporarily.

7. To make the choker, measure the neck and add two inches. Cut a piece of wire this length and use a large coffee can, jug, or bottle as a form around which to bend the wire into a circle. Work the wire until you have a good circle; then remove it from the form and forge ½ inch of each wire end flat. File off rough edges and bend the wire back to form hooks (illustration A). Bend hooks at right angles to each other for best fit; then forge choker wire all around in an even pattern to help it keep its shape.

8. Thread beads onto plain wire attached to the brass semicircle. Allowing for a loop, trim off excess wire and make an open loop with roundnose pliers. Slip the loop onto the choker wire and close the loop.

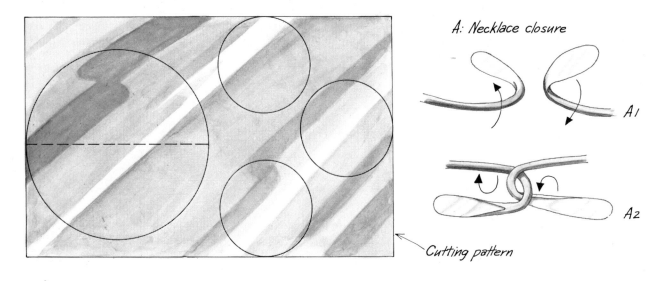

A: Necklace closure

A1

A2

Cutting pattern

Seashells and Silver Necklace

(Color photo on page 28)

The bounty of the ocean and your own ingenuity provide the raw materials for this necklace. Clam, mollusk, abalone, and other seashells join hand-fashioned paper beads as well as purchased silver tubing and beads to adorn your neck with beach colors and textures. Substitute coiled wire for the tubes if they prove difficult to find, or use hollow shells, copper tubing, or wound paper tubes instead. Instructions for making wound paper beads are given below; to make tubes, cut untapered strips of paper one inch wide and roll them up as shown.

Equipment: Roundnose pliers, wire cutters, hand drill and ⅛-inch drill bit, large blunt tapestry needle.

Materials: 78 white clamshell hishi beads (small white pearl buttons may be substituted), four dentilium or tusk shells, four rolled paper beads (see step 1 below), two ¾-inch lengths of sterling silver tubing, one large seashell (a giant white chiton is used here), four abalone shell buttons, two abalone-shell beads (or substitute small to medium-sized shells), two abalone-shell fragments (sold in hobby shops for mosaic table tops), three ½-inch-diameter sterling silver beads, one commercial necklace clasp, 15 inches of 20-gauge copper wire, eight inches of 24-gauge sterling silver wire, white glue.

How to Make

1. Make four rolled paper beads by cutting long triangles (¾ inch at large end, ⅛ inch at small end, and 12 inches in length) from the shiny, color-printed pages of a large-format magazine or the Sunday comic strip papers, or use very old or antique magazines and newspapers for a special yellow "patina." The longer and more tapered the triangle cut, the fatter the bead. Any number of variations can be worked using this simple approach: place the paper triangle with its right side *face down* and place the tapestry needle at the widest end of the triangle (illustration A). Roll the end tightly around the needle; then roll up the paper, working away from yourself and toward the small end of the triangle. Keep the roll as tight as possible. When you are finished, glue the free end of the triangle with white glue. Make four paper beads, setting them aside until later.

2. Bend the 15-inch length of copper wire around a circular oatmeal box, large glass jar, or some other circular form to create a round choker band. At one end, make a loop with the roundnose pliers (illustration B).

3. String beads and shells onto the necklace in this order: one tusk shell, six hishi, one tusk shell, six hishi, one large-diameter paper bead, six hishi, one sterling tube, six hishi, one small-diameter paper bead, six hishi, one abalone-shell button, three hishi, one abalone-shell button, three hishi, one silver bead, one abalone-shell fragment (drill hole through fragment with hand drill). This completes half of the necklace. For the second half, begin with another abalone-shell fragment and work backward, ending with one tusk shell. Make a loop at the end of the choker with pliers; cut off any excess wire.

4. Add the shell dangle by bending the 8-inch length of 24-gauge sterling wire in half and looping the wire over the choker between the two abalone-shell fragments (illustration C). Thread both ends of the wire down through both abalone-shell beads and one round sterling bead.

5. Drill a hole with the hand drill near the top of the shell dangle and pass both ends of the wire through it from front to back. Make a loop by wrapping both ends of wire around themselves above the shell dangle. Press down protruding wire ends with pliers.

6. Attach a commercial necklace clasp to the loop at the top of the choker band, with pliers.

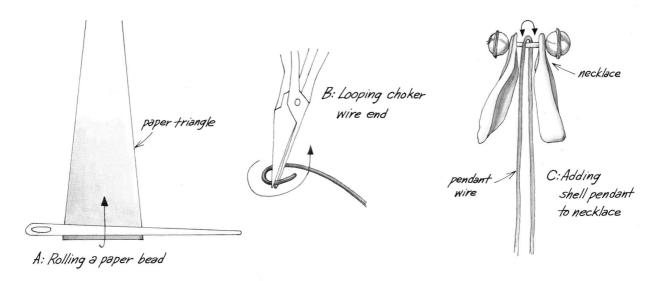

paper triangle

A: Rolling a paper bead

B: Looping choker wire end

necklace

pendant wire

C: Adding shell pendant to necklace

Necklace of Feathers and Knots

(Color photo on page 29)

Macramé and feathers create a soft, lacelike necklace in shades of blue grey and ecru. Definitely something for the person who has had previous experience with macramé, this project incorporates a number of advanced knots worked with clean precision.

Equipment: 12-inch by 12-inch square of composition board, one box of T-pins and glass-headed pins, scissors, tape measure, single-blade razor.

Materials: 52 yards, 8 inches of grey #18 waxed nylon cord; 15 yards, 12 inches of ecru #18 waxed nylon cord; 12 small brown and black feathers; 19 small carved olivewood beads; one 1½-inch-diameter black glass or plastic ring; white glue.

How to Make

1. To make the pendant portion of the neckpiece, cut eleven 40-inch-long strands of grey cord; then cut a 120-inch length from the ecru cord. Fold the grey cords in half and mount them onto the ring as shown on page 19. This will give you 22 working cords. Pin the ring to your working board to hold it secure. Divide the 22 working cords into two equal groups and mark the point of division with a pin. Fold the ecru cord in half and pin it to the board by the ring at the point of division.

2. Using the ecru cord as a holding cord and the grey mounted cords as working cords, work double half hitch knots out from the center in both directions until the last working cord on each side has been used; then work horizontal double half hitches back toward the center where you began (illustration A).

3. Work vertical double half hitch knots out from the center on both sides and back again, using the ecru cord as the working cord and the grey cords as holding cords. You will end up back at the center.

4. Repeat step 2.

5. Thread a bead onto the four center cords (two ecru and two grey); then tie six vertical reverse double half hitches (see page 19) with the next four cords on either side. Thread a bead onto the next group of four cords on each side, tying eight vertical reverse double half hitches with the remaining four cords on each outside edge.

6. Repeat step 2.

7. Repeat step 3.

8. To attach feathers, trim the shaft of a feather to about ½ inch and clean off any fuzz. Lay the shaft of the trimmed feather along the ecru holding cord with the feather's head pointing to the left. Tie a row of horizontal double half hitches with the grey cords, working from the center to the left-hand edge and tying over the feather shaft and the ecru holding cord at the same time. Repeat for the right side of the pendant.

9. Using the ecru cords as the working cords and the grey cords as the holding cords, tie one row of vertical double half hitches back to the center. Repeat for the right side.

10. Using the grey cords as working cords and the ecru cord as a holding cord, tie a row of horizontal double half hitches out to the left-hand edge. Repeat for the right side.

11. Repeat step 9.

12. Repeat step 8.

13. Repeat step 10 but work from edges to center.

14. Working from the outside left-hand edge, tie eight vertical reverse double half hitches (see page 19) with the first *two* cords. With the next two cords, tie only six of these knots. The next pair of cords will have four knots, the next pair will have three, and the last pair will have two vertical reverse double half hitches. Work the right-hand side in the same way, starting with the outside right-hand edge and working in toward the center. When you've finished, there will be two grey cords and two ecru holding cords left free at the very center.

15. Cross the ecru cords and pin them each at a 45° angle. Using these pinned cords as holding cords, tie a diagonal row of double half hitches, starting with the two free center grey cords and working from the center to the outside left-hand edge. Repeat for the right-hand side. At the end of each diagonal row, tie each ecru holding cord into a tight knot, snip off excess cord, and dip each knot into white glue to hold it securely.

16. Cross the two free center grey cords as in step 15 and pin to the board at a 45° angle, parallel to the preceding diagonal rows. Lay the shaft of a trimmed feather along the holding cord and complete as outlined in step 8. Repeat for right-hand side of pendant. Knot the holding cords, trim off excess, and dip knots into white glue.

17. Slide a bead over the five outside cords on each side and tie each group of five as one into an overhand knot below the bead. Trim off excess cords and glue the knots. Slide two beads over the remaining center cords and tie them as one into an overhand knot. Trim off excess cords and glue; then insert the trimmed shafts of two feathers into the beads, covering the knot.

To make two matching neckpieces for the necklace, work through the following instructions two separate times, placing the feathers in the left-hand neckpiece with their heads on the left side and the feathers in the right-hand neckpiece with their heads on the right side.

18. Cut six cords, each 120 inches long, from the grey cord and two cords, each 216 inches long, from the ecru cord. As shown on page 19, fold and mount these cords onto the ring to make 12 working cords.

19. Fold the ecru cord in half and, dividing the mounted grey cords into two equal groups, pin the fold of the ecru cord at the point of division (refer to step 1).

20. Repeat step 2.

21. Repeat step 3.

22. Repeat step 2.

23. Thread a bead onto the two center ecru holding cords; then tie six vertical reverse double half hitches, using only the next two cords (refer to page 19) on each side of the bead. Thread a bead onto the next pair of two cords on each side. Then tie eight vertical reverse double half hitches with the remaining pair of two cords on each side.

24. Repeat step 2.

25. Repeat step 3.

26. Repeat step 8, omitting the last sentence.

27. Repeat step 9, omitting the last sentence.

28. Repeat step 10, omitting the last sentence.

29. Repeat step 9, omitting the last sentence.

30. Repeat step 8, omitting the last sentence.

31. Repeat step 10 but work from edges to center.

32. Working from the outside left-hand edge, tie six vertical reverse double half hitches (refer to page 19) with the first *two* cords. With the next two cords, tie only four of these knots (the last pair of cords will have two vertical reverse double half hitches). Work the right-hand side in the same way, starting from the outside right-hand edge and working in toward the center. This should use up all but the two center ecru holding cords.

33. Cross the ecru cords and pin them each at a 45° angle. Using these pinned cords as holding cords, tie a diagonal row of double half hitches, using the grey cords as working cords and working from the center to the outside left-hand edge. Repeat for the right-hand side.

34. Cross the two center grey cords and pin them each at a 45° angle and parallel to the previous rows. Using these as holding cords, tie a second diagonal row of double half hitches, using the remaining grey cords as working cords. At the end of the row, use the ecru cord to make the final double half hitch knot. Repeat for the right-hand side.

35. Thread a bead onto the four center grey cords; then pin the grey holding cords from the second diagonal rows in step 34 at a 45° angle back toward the center of the neck piece (illustration B); tie a diagonal row of double half hitches back toward the center from each outside edge. Use the ecru cords at the very outside edges to tie the first knots.

36. As in step 35, pin both outside ecru cords at a 45° angle in toward the center and use them as holding cords to tie a second diagonal row of double half hitches coming in from each side and meeting at the center.

37. Repeat step 32 but tie *eight* vertical reverse double half hitches with the first two cords, *five* knots with the second pair of cords and *two* knots with the last pair of cords. Repeat for the right-hand side.

38. Repeat step 33.

39. Repeat step 34 but *do not* use the ecru cord for the final outside knot. This will leave five grey working cords coming in toward the center from each side. Using the three center cords on each side as holding cords, tie a square knot (see page 19) with the two outside cords as working cords. You will have a diagonally placed square knot on each side (illustration C).

40. To make a berry knot, pin the first cord on the right-hand side at a 45° angle pointing toward the lower left. This will form a holding cord for a diagonal row of double half hitches, using all five cords from the square knot on the left-hand side as working cords. Repeat with the second, third, fourth, and fifth cords from the right-hand square knot. When you finish, there will be five diagonal rows of knots pointing toward the lower left, with two groups of five grey cords each pointing diagonally off to the left and to the right. As in step 39, tie each group of five into a diagonally placed square knot with three cords as holding cords and two as working cords. The tighter each knot is tied, the more rounded the berry.

41. Using the grey holding cords on either side of the berry knot as holding cords and the groups of five cords as working cords, tie a diagonal row of double half hitches meeting at the center below the berry. Repeat for the remaining two outside ecru holding cords.

42. Repeat step 32 but tie *11* vertical reverse double half hitches with the first two cords, *six* knots with the second pair of cords, and *two* knots with the last pair of cords. Repeat for the right-hand side.

43. Repeat the bead and berry sequence (steps 33 through 42) two more times.

44. Repeat steps 33 and 34; then group all grey cords together as holding cords and use the two ecru cords as tying cords to make six square knots. When these knots have been tied, start to cut off two grey cords from the bunch of holding cords after every other square knot tied until four grey cords and two ecru cords are left.

45. Divide the cords into three equal groups and braid them until the chain is long enough to make a tie at the back of the neck. Tie all ends as one in an overhand knot, trim off excess cords, and glue the knot.

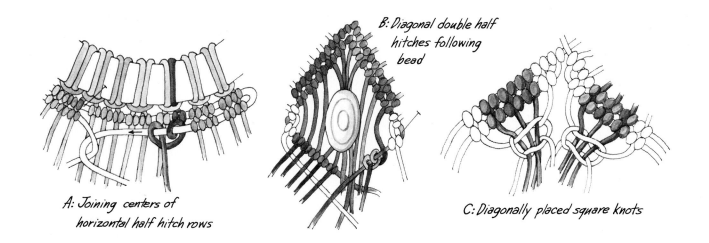

A: Joining centers of horizontal half hitch rows

B: Diagonal double half hitches following bead

C: Diagonally placed square knots

Oaxaca Choker (page 22)

Mexican geometric design is elegantly worked in Cavandoli (or pattern) macramé knotting. Design: Edwina Hawbecker.

Trade Bead Necklace (page 24)

Primitive styling combines hand-forged discs with African trade beads to make this necklace. Design: Leslie Correll.

Sea Shells and Silver Necklace (page 25)

Shades of the sea: abalone, clam, and tusk shell beads and buttons, punctuated with silver beads and antique hand-rolled paper beads, make a necklace that's an echo of the ocean. Design: Pat Deardorff.

Exotic Hardwoods Necklace (page 31)

Exotic berbinga, osage orange, and walnut hardwoods give color and character to this unusual wooden necklace. Lamination gives the striped effect. Design: Izetta Feeny.

Necklace of Feathers and Knots (page 26)

Intricate macramé tracery flows gracefully down into a soft burst of feathers in this dramatically designed body jewelry necklace. Design: Barbara De Oca.

Chain of Beads Necklace (page 30)

Catch two falling stars and tie them at the ends of this subtly colored and knotted ceramic bead and linen cord necklace. The beads are all handmade by you. Design: Valery Guignon.

Chain of Beads Necklace

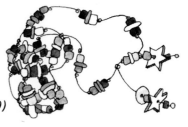

(Color photo on page 29)

Here's a simple yet elegant project well within the means of just about anyone. If you have access to a ceramic kiln, you could make the beads from porcelain and stoneware clays colored with such oxides as chrome (green), cobalt (blue), and iron (red, black, or brown, depending on the amount used), putting them through a bisque firing to harden them and to set their colors. Otherwise, use the method described below.

Equipment: Scissors, round wooden toothpick, rubber gloves, breadboard, art knife.

Materials: One batch of kitchen clay (recipe on page 6), one package *each* of black, blue green, brown, and terracotta commercial powdered cold water fabric dye, 4½ feet of #18 waxed linen or cotton macramé cord, white beach sand (optional), seven small plastic bags and ties.

How to Make

1. Divide the kitchen clay into seven equal balls. Wearing rubber gloves, flatten one ball of clay onto the breadboard and pour a small amount of black powdered dye onto the clay. Blend the powder and clay by kneading them until well mixed. Continue to add dye and to knead together until you get the desired shade.

2. Do the same for the remaining three colors. You will have three balls of kitchen clay left. Set one of these remaining balls aside; then knead a *very small* amount of blue dye into another of the remaining balls until you have a pastel blue color. Using the brown dye, do the same with the last ball of kitchen clay to make a pale brown shade. You should have seven separate colors: black, light brown, dark brown, light blue, dark blue, white, and terracotta. Put each ball of clay into its own plastic bag and seal tightly, squeezing out all air before sealing. Keep the clay covered in this way when it isn't being used, to prevent it from drying out. Using the following procedures, make the beads for the necklace.

3. For round beads, pull off a small amount of clay and form it into a small ball about the size of a peppercorn. Insert the pointed end of the toothpick into the

ball until it begins to protrude on the other side of the ball. Remove it and turn the ball around, reinserting the toothpick into the small hole left where it protruded from the ball in the first place. Push the ball of clay onto the toothpick until a good-sized hole has been made. Check the bead holes against the diameter of the waxed cord to make sure they are correctly sized.

4. For flat beads, make a ball of clay the size of a peppercorn; press it down flat with your fingertip onto the wooden surface of the breadboard. Use the toothpick to make a circular hole in the center of each bead by moving it in a circular motion. If possible, leave the beads in place until they dry. If not, carefully remove them by sliding a sheet of paper under the beads to separate them from the wood.

5. To make the stars, press a ½-inch-diameter ball of clay flat until it is about ⅛ inch thick. With the tip of the toothpick, trace out a ½-inch-high, five-pointed star. Cut it out with the art knife and put a hole through its center with the toothpick. Allow it to remain on the board until dry.

6. To make the necklace, first make the following number of beads: 7 flat, 12 round, and 2 star-shaped white beads; 10 flat and 7 round light blue beads; 2 flat and 12 round dark blue beads; 2 flat terra-cotta beads; 8 round black beads; 3 flat and 10 round light brown beads; 5 flat and 6 round dark brown beads. Allow the beads to dry overnight. If you like, you can mix a little white beach sand with the brown shades of clay to make it look like stoneware clay.

7. To start stringing the beads, tie an overhand knot about 4 inches up from one end of the waxed cord. Thread the beads on in the order given in the illustration below, knotting once before each group and once after. Space the bead groups about ½ inch to ¾ inch apart, varying the spacing to give the necklace a random look.

8. Before threading beads on the two dangling cord ends, tie a square knot (see page 19) about 3 inches up from the ends of the cords. Then thread on the remaining beads in this order: one flat light blue, one flat white, one round light brown, one star, one round dark brown, on one cord; and one flat white, one round light blue, one star, and one round dark brown, on the other. Tie a knot below the beads on each cord end to hold the beads in place. Trim off excess cord.

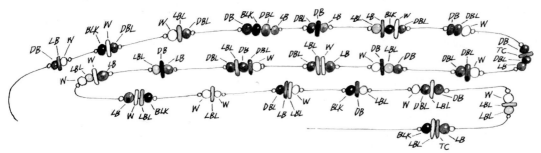

DB: Dark brown
LB: Light brown
W: White
BLK: Black
LBL: Light blue
DBL: Dark blue
TC: Terracotta
—o—: Knot

Exotic Hardwoods Necklace

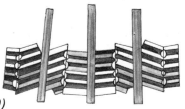

(Color photo on page 29)

Rare and exotic woods give character to this pendant necklace, but other hardwoods may be colored with fabric dye (see page 11) and used instead, if these are unavailable.

Equipment: Scrolling, jig, or power saw; sanding block; four grades of garnet sandpaper from 100 to 250; hand drill; ¼-inch drill bit; ³⁄₁₆-inch drill bit; #70 drill bit; wire cutters; roundnose pliers; two 3-inch by 3-inch by 1-inch blocks of scrap wood; one medium-sized C-clamp; soft cloth; tracing paper; art knife; ruler; steel wool.

Materials: One 2-inch by 1-inch by 1-inch rectangle *each* of three different hardwoods (Osage orange, berbinga, and walnut are used here), one 5-inch length of ³⁄₁₆-inch-diameter wooden dowel, one 4-inch length of ¼-inch-diameter wooden dowel, ½-inch by ³⁄₁₆-inch by 12-inch length of Osage orange (or equivalent hardwood), ³⁄₁₆-inch by ⅛-inch by 23-inch length of berbinga (or equivalent hardwood), 20 inches of 26-gauge brass or copper wire, 2-inch by 6½-inch by ⅛-inch piece of hardwood, wood glue, wood oil or clear sealer with brush and thinner, rubber cement, commercial necklace clasp.

How to Make

1. Cut a 12-inch length of Osage orange into 12 equal segments and sand all surfaces smooth. Then cut the 22½-inch length of berbinga into the following lengths: 3⅞ inches, 4⅛ inches, 3⅞ inches, and six lengths each measuring 1¾ inches long. Sand surfaces smooth.

2. Cut three slices of Osage orange, two measuring 2 inches by 1 inch by ⅛ inch and one measuring 2 inches by 1 inch by ³⁄₁₆ inch. Be sure to cut *across* the grain of the wood when cutting all pieces. Next, cut three slices of berbinga in the same sizes as the Osage orange. Finally, cut five slices of walnut, three measuring 2 inches by 1 inch by ³⁄₁₆ inch, and two measuring 2 inches by 1 inch by ⅛ inch.

3. Using a sanding block clamped to the work bench, sand the surfaces of each slice of wood until smooth. Then, using a waterproof wood glue, glue and stack the slices in the following order: ³⁄₁₆-inch Osage orange, ³⁄₁₆-inch walnut, ⅛-inch Osage orange, ³⁄₁₆-inch walnut, ⅛-inch Osage orange, ³⁄₁₆-inch walnut, ⅛-inch berbinga, ⅛-inch walnut, ⅛-inch berbinga, ⅛-inch walnut, ³⁄₁₆-inch berbinga. Clamp the "sandwich" tightly between two pieces of scrap wood and allow it to dry for at least 12 hours to insure a strong bond.

4. When the stacked slices are dry, release them from the clamp and sand all edges until they are smooth and even. This should make a block of wood measuring about 1¾ inches high, 2 inches wide, and 1 inch deep. Sawing *across* the laminated slices of wood (illustration A), cut the block into two equal pieces, each measuring 1¾ inches high, 2 inches wide, and ½ inch deep.

5. Trace the patterns below onto tracing paper, cut them out carefully with an art knife and ruler, and glue one pattern to the surface of each rectangle of wood.

6. Clamp one of the wood rectangles firmly but not tightly to the scrap wood and, with the proper drill bits, drill holes as indicated in the pattern. Repeat for the

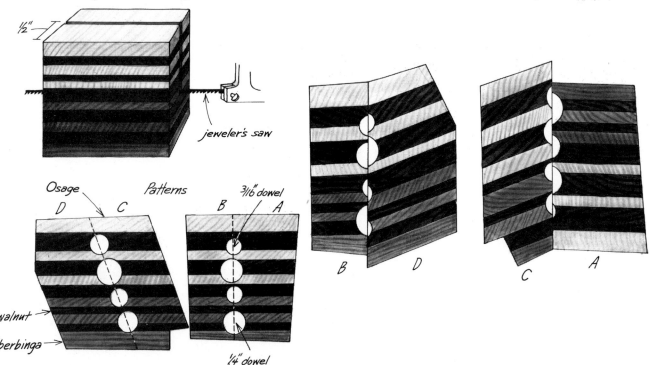

½"

jeweler's saw

Osage   Patterns   ³⁄₁₆" dowel

D   C   B   A

walnut

berbinga

¼" dowel

B   D   C   A

second block of wood. Cut the 5-inch length of ³⁄₁₆-inch-diameter doweling into five equal lengths, coat them with glue, and work them into the drilled holes. Don't force them; if fit is too tight, ream out the holes again.

7. Cut the 4-inch length of ¼-inch-diameter wooden dowel into four equal lengths, coat them with glue, and work them into drilled holes as in step 6.

8. Allow dowels to dry for at least 12 hours; then cut off protruding ends of dowels on both sides of both pieces. Saw around the outlines of both pieces, following glued-down tracing paper patterns.

9. Next, slice down through the dowels as indicated by the dotted line on each pattern. Sand all cut surfaces until they are smooth and even. Then glue pieces back together as shown in illustration B, keeping the circles slightly off center. Clamp firmly and allow to dry for 12 hours.

10. When they are dry, cut two ¼-inch-thick slices from *each* block, slicing down through the sandwiched layers. This will give two matched pieces from each block. Sand all cut edges and surfaces until they are smooth and even.

11. Following the order shown in the photograph on page 29, glue the slices of laminated wood to the three longest lengths of berbinga. When the glue has set, place the entire piece over the 2-inch by 6½-inch by ⅛-inch piece of hardwood and trace the outline of the pendant onto the hardwood. Cut out this backing and sand all surfaces. Glue the pendant to the backing and allow it to dry.

12. With a #70 drill bit, drill holes into both ends of each ½-inch length of Osage orange and each 1¾-inch length of berbinga. Then cut 38 ½-inch lengths of 26-gauge wire and bend one end of each length into a circle with the roundnose pliers. Glue the other ends into the drilled holes in the Osage and berbinga pieces. Link the pieces together, alternating Osage with berbinga and placing three Osage pieces at the ends of each half of the chain. Attach the commercial clasp to the last piece of Osage orange on one half of the chain.

13. Using the photo on page 29 as a guide, attach the chain to the pendant by drilling into the berbinga posts, gluing in links, and attaching them to the ends of the chain. After allowing glue to dry, coat wood with wood oil or clear sealer. When the finish is dry, buff it with fine steel wool.

Officer's Ribbon Tie Bar

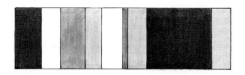

(Color photo on page 36)

Though it appears to be the genuine article, this officer's ribbon tie bar is actually only a copy worked with colored embroidery floss that is wrapped around a cardboard rectangle and glued into place. If you want to be authentic, check your local library for books giving information on the meanings of various color bar combinations.

Equipment: Art knife, pencil, ruler.

Materials: ½-inch by 1½-inch rectangle of lightweight cardboard; one skein *each* of dark blue, medium blue, light blue, and tan 6-strand embroidery floss; white glue; commercial tie clip backing.

How to Make

1. Cut a rectangle of cardboard measuring 1¼ inches by ⁵⁄₁₆ inches with the art knife. Coat half of the rectangle with glue, both front and back.

2. Cut a 10-inch length from each color of floss and separate one strand of floss from each group of six. Mark the rectangle into the following divisions: ³⁄₁₆ inch, ³⁄₃₂ inch, ⁵⁄₃₂ inch, ¹⁄₁₆ inch, ⅛ inch, ¹⁄₁₆ inch, ⅛ inch, ⅜ inch, ¹⁄₁₆ inch.

3. Begin to cover the rectangle by pressing one loose end of the dark blue floss into the glue on the back of the cardboard. When strand is anchored, start to wind the floss around the cardboard carefully, laying each strand as close to the preceding strand as possible (illustration A). Wind the color on until ³⁄₁₆ inch has been covered; then cut and anchor the thread end in the glue on the back.

4. Continue to wind on colors as indicated in illustration B, adding glue as necessary. Avoid getting glue on the floss.

5. When you've finished, coat the back of the cardboard with glue to hold all floss securely. Then set the tie bar face into the glue, centering it on the rectangle. Allow it to dry overnight before using it.

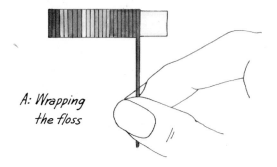

A: Wrapping the floss

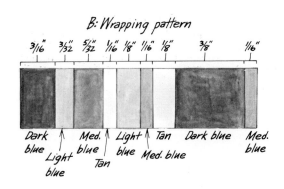

B: Wrapping pattern

3/16" 3/32" 5/32" 1/16" 1/8" 1/16" 1/8" 3/8" 1/16"

Dark blue   Med. blue   Light blue   Tan   Dark blue   Med. blue
Light blue   Tan   Med. blue

Teak and Silver Tie Tack

(Color photo on page 36)

A very distinctive yet inexpensive birthday or Father's Day gift, this cut-silver and teak tie tack requires a sure hand with the jeweler's saw and drill. If silver is unavailable, use thin copper or brass sheet metal for the cut-out portion of the tie tack. If hardwoods are unavailable, a softwood (such as pine) may be used if it has first been stained and sanded smooth.

Equipment: Jeweler's saw, bench pin, hand drill, ½₂-inch drill bit, ¼-inch drill bit, two pieces of scrap wood, one 3-inch C-clamp, half-round jeweler's file, square jeweler's file, tripoli, jeweler's rouge and soft rag, tracing paper, carbon paper, pencil, ruler, wooden toothpick, scribing tool, #150 sandpaper.

Materials: A ½-inch by ¾-inch by ⅛-inch rectangle of hardwood (teak is used here), a ½-inch by ¾-inch rectangle of 26-gauge silver sheet, one commercial tie tack backing, jewelry cement, epoxy glue.

How to Make

1. Copy design below onto tracing paper and transfer to surface of silver sheet, with carbon paper. Scribe design into surface with a sharp pin or other tool.

2. With ⅛₆-inch drill bit, drill a hole through each area to be removed from the silver sheet (illustration A). Loosen and remove the end of the saw blade nearest to the handle of the saw and pass the blade through one of the drilled holes with the scribed side of the silver facing away from the saw handle (illustration B). Re-fasten the saw blade (see page 15).

3. Cut out the drilled area, moving slowly to keep the blade on the scribed lines. When one drilled area has been cut, move the blade to another as explained in step 2. Continue until all areas to be removed have been cut out.

4. With square or half-round files, remove rough spots and burrs from all edges, inside and outside. Polish the cut silver with red jeweler's rouge and a soft rag or a buffing wheel (see page 16).

5. Sand all edges and both faces of the hardwood rectangle until fairly smooth. Buff the wood with tripoli until all surfaces become darker and slightly glossy.

6. On the back of the hardwood rectangle, mark the center and drill a shallow hole with the ¼-inch drill at the point marked.

7. To attach the cut-silver design to the face of the wood, lightly coat the back of the silver with jewelry cement. A toothpick can be used to pick up and to spread the cement thinly.

8. Clamp the silver and wooden rectangle between two pieces of soft scrap wood with a 3-inch C-clamp and allow to dry for several hours.

9. When the glued silver and wood rectangle has dried, mix up a small batch of epoxy and, with a toothpick, place a small amount in the drilled hole and on the face of the tie tack backing. When the epoxy has become tacky (which happens quickly), press the face of the tie tack backing into the epoxy on the wooden rectangle, straightening the backing until it is perpendicular to the wooden rectangle. Allow it to dry overnight.

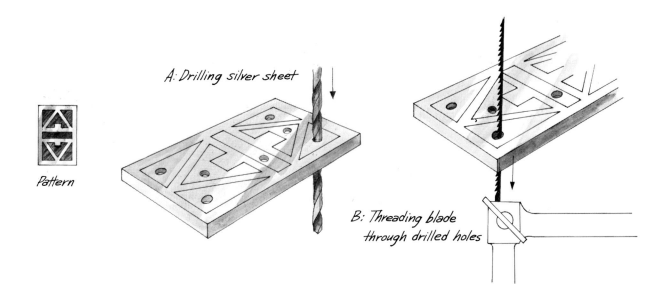

Pattern

A: Drilling silver sheet

B: Threading blade through drilled holes

Coral Clasp Tie Bar

(Color photo on page 36)

Have you ever picked up shells and driftwood from the beach or small pebbles from the forest floor as mementos of an enjoyable vacation? Here's a way to get that keepsake out of hiding: make it into an attractive tie clasp that can be enjoyed by both the wearer and the appreciative viewer.

Equipment: Bench pin (see page 12), equaling needle file (or carpenter's flat hand file), jeweler's saw, jeweler's rouge and soft cloth, roundnose pliers, metal snips, small ruler and pencil, wire cutters.

Materials: A 1½-inch by 2-inch rectangle of 25-gauge sheet silver (the size of the sheet will vary, depending on the size and shape of the item used to decorate the clasp), commercial tie bar backing, one piece of rough sea coral (or any other shell, stone, or material for decoration), jewelry cement.

How to Make

1. With pencil and ruler, mark the center of each edge of the rectangle of sheet silver, as well as the center of the rectangle itself.

2. Draw the outlines for the backing prongs with a scribing tool as shown in illustration A and connect them to form a diamond-shaped center.

3. Cut out the pronged diamond shape with the jeweler's saw, supporting the work on the bench pin and cutting slowly to avoid bending the metal.

4. When the shape is cut out, snip a sharp point at the end of each prong with a metal snip (illustration B). File the sharp tips and all edges to remove burrs and to smooth edges. Polish the silver with red jeweler's rouge and a soft cloth.

5. Place the rough coral (or other item) over the diamond-shaped center of the prongs. With roundnose pliers, bend pointed prong ends as shown in illustration C. Then bend prongs up and around coral or stone with the pliers, turning the prong points into the surface of the coral or stone and adjusting all four until the coral is held securely.

6. With red jeweler's rouge and a soft cloth, carefully polish the four prongs.

7. Apply a thin layer of jewelry cement to the face of the tie clasp backing and allow it to become slightly tacky. Do the same for the diamond-shaped backing of the prongs.

8. Press the two tacky surfaces together and align the clasp with the backing, making sure the clasp is well hidden behind the coral or stone. Allow it to dry overnight.

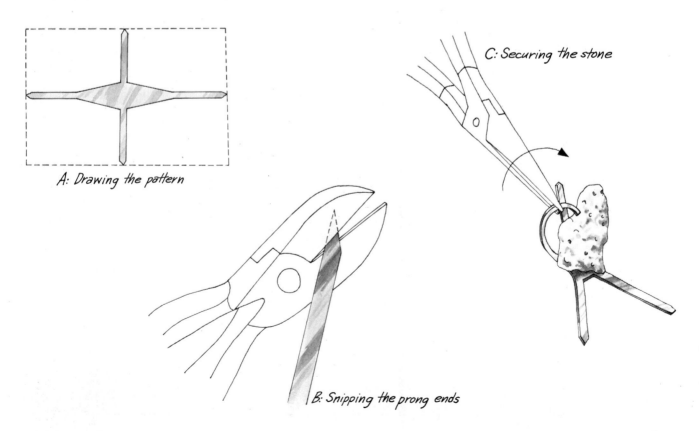

A: Drawing the pattern

B: Snipping the prong ends

C: Securing the stone

Painted Leather Barrettes

(Color photo on page 37)

Cut from scrap leather, these barrettes are inexpensive and easy to make — yet they show a lively, attractive face to the world. Let your imagination take off and create individualized hair clips with favorite flowers, animals, symbols, or the name of the wearer. The only special piece of equipment you'll need is the leatherworker's swivel knife as shown below. Practice with it first before starting the project.

Equipment: Swivel knife, art knife, ruler, pencil, ballpoint pen, tracing paper, wool dauber (a piece of lamb's wool), #00 camel's hair brush, wooden toothpick.

Materials: 1½-inch by 2½-inch rectangle of 6 or 8-ounce latigo leather for each pair of barrettes to be made; one bottle *each* of acrylic-base red, yellow, blue, green, brown, and white leather paints; clear plastic spray; plastic-base craft cement; one pair of commercial barrette backings.

How to Make

1. Copy one of the patterns below onto tracing paper; then dampen the surface of the leather rectangle with a sponge and transfer the design to the leather by going over the tracing with a ballpoint pen. Remember to do this twice, once for each barrette. Then, following the traced outlines, cut out leather rectangles for each barrette with an art knife and a ruler.

2. When the pattern is traced onto the leather, use the swivel knife to cut the pattern into the leather. If you aren't sure of how to use a swivel knife, practice first on a piece of scrap leather (illustration A).

3. With a piece of lamb's wool, daub a water-thinned but even coat of the background color over the entire piece, both front and back. Allow it to dry for an hour or more. A second coat may be necessary to completely color the leather. Again, allow an hour or more for drying time.

4. To apply the actual design, use a #00 camel's hair brush and full strength paint. Two or three coats may be necessary to cover a dark background. If so, allow the paint to dry thoroughly between applications. When it's completely dry, spray on a protective coat of clear plastic to prevent moisture and chipping from damaging your design.

5. When paints and spray coating are completely dry, apply a thin coating of glue to the face of the barrette backing and to the back of the leather rectangle with a toothpick. When tacky, press both glued sides together. Allow the barrette to dry overnight before wearing it.

Patterns

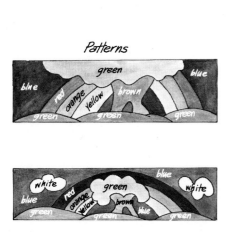

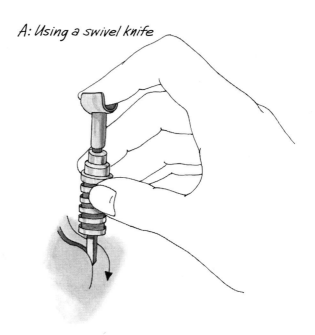

A: Using a swivel knife

Officer's Ribbon Tie Bar (page 32)

Earn your stripes by making a tie bar in the form of an officer's ribbon decoration. Each stripe has its own meaning. Design: Alyson Smith Gonsalves.

Teak and Silver Tie Tack (page 33)

Tack your tie into place with a bit of teak and silver; its simple good looks make this tie tack compatible with any tie pattern, be it sporty or dressy. Design: Alyson Smith Gonsalves.

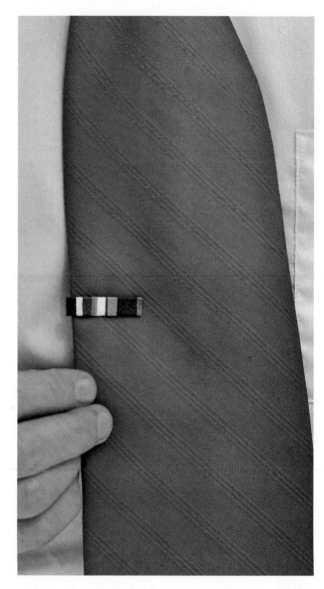

Coral Clasp Tie Bar (page 34)

Coral tie clip is simple to make, yet looks like a very expensive piece of custom jewelry. Semi-precious stones can be substituted for the coral, if desired. Design: Alyson Smith Gonsalves.

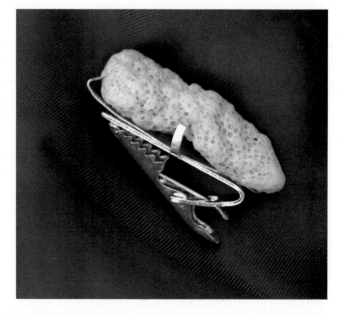

Painted Leather Barrettes (page 35)

Clip your hair back with one of these unusual hand-painted leather barrettes. Easy to make, they're each cut from leather scrap. Design: Shirley Pilkington.

Macrame Name Bracelet (page 39)

Alphabet baby beads are joined by simple macramé knots to form a name chain bracelet in shades of black and white. These make good personalized gifts. Design: Luisita Amiguet.

Peach Pit Bracelet (page 38)

A polished peach pit provides the focal point of this simple bead and thong bracelet. Copper wire is used to bind the beads in place. Design: Alyson Smith Gonsalves.

Peach Pit Bracelet

(Color photo on page 37)

A simple bracelet for casual wear can be made from a bit of copper wire, some black leather thong or cord, glass beads, and the pit of a peach, apricot, or plum. Cleaned, sanded down, and polished, the pits can become surprisingly interesting beads. A simple hook and eye set (used for sewing projects) forms the bracelet clasp.

Equipment: Roundnose pliers, wire cutters, #80 and #100 sandpaper, hand drill, ¼-inch drill bit, bench vise, small paintbrush, small ruler.

Materials: 32 inches of 26-gauge copper wire; two 8-inch lengths of thin black leather thong (or lightweight dark waxed linen cord); two peach-colored, ⅜-inch-diameter glass beads with large center holes; one peach or apricot pit; shellac or varnish; paint thinner; large black garment hook and eye.

How to Make

1. Clean the fruit pit by scrubbing off any fleshy residue with a stiff bristle brush and soap. Dry the pit and then sand off the sharp point on each end with #80 sandpaper. Clamp the pit into the jaws of the bench vise and drill through it from one sanded end to the other (illustration A). Remove the pit and sand surfaces with #100 sandpaper until smooth. With a small brush, coat the pit with shellac or varnish. Use paint thinner to clean brush afterwards and allow pit to dry.

2. To assemble the bracelet, first pass both lengths of thong through the pit, keeping their ends as even as possible.

3. Next, pass one thong down through the top hole of one of the glass beads and the other thong up through the bottom hole (illustration B). Do the same for the other glass bead on the other side of the pit. Then center the pit and beads on the two lengths of thong, still keeping the thong ends even.

4. Measure and cut two 8-inch lengths of copper wire. Bend one end of one piece of wire at a right angle and lay it next to one of the glass beads along the two thongs (illustration C), then wrap the wire tightly around both thongs, moving away from the glass bead. Wrap until wire is all used but ¼ inch at the end. With roundnose pliers, bend the wire down and tuck it down between the two leather thongs (illustration D). Do the same with the other glass bead, thongs, and piece of wire.

5. Put the bracelet on your wrist and wrap the thongs around to the back to judge where to attach the hook and eye for correct fit (the bracelet should not be too loose or it will fall off). With roundnose pliers, enlarge the attachment holes of the hook and the eye by slightly spreading the wires until they open up. Thread one thong through each hole; then close the wires.

6. Double the thongs back on themselves and wrap them both with an 8-inch length of copper wire as in step 4. Trim off excess thong.

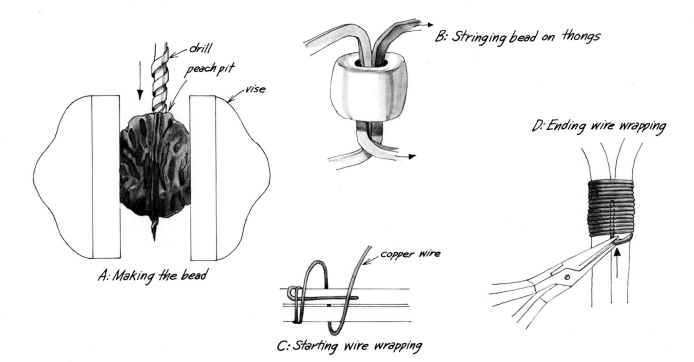

A: Making the bead

B: Stringing bead on thongs

C: Starting wire wrapping

D: Ending wire wrapping

Macrame Name Bracelet

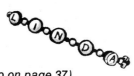

(Color photo on page 37)

Based on the idea of the baby's bracelet (you may still have one from your infancy), the name bracelet makes a good personalized gift for a friend or relative. Only one macramé knot, the square knot, is used to make the bracelet, which is finished off with braided chains at either end.

Equipment: A 12-inch by 12-inch square of composition board (Celotex), one box of T-pins or glass-headed pins, scissors, tape measure.

Materials: Alphabet beads with letters of the name to be put on the bracelet, one tube of white Indian seed beads, two ¼-inch-diameter white plastic or glass beads, two 30-inch-long strands of #18 black waxed nylon cord, one 15-inch strand of #18 white waxed nylon cord, white glue.

How to Make

1. Fold all three strands in half to find their center points and pin the centers to your working board in this order: black above, white in the center, black below. Pin them to the board with ½ inch of space between each strand.

2. Slide the middle letter (or one of the two middle letters) onto the white cord (which will be called the holding cord) and tie a square knot (illustration A) to the left of the letter bead with the two black cords (called tying cords). Slide a seed bead onto the holding cord and up to the square knot; then hold it in place by tying another square knot below it with the black tying cords.

3. Slide the preceding letter of the name onto the holding cord and follow the procedure outlined in step 2 until all letters of the first part of the name (those falling to the left of the center letter) have been attached. Follow the last alphabet bead with a square knot; then pass another seed bead onto the holding cord and secure it with a square knot.

4. Next, thread a single seed bead onto each black tying cord and secure by following them with another square knot; then tie a second square knot slightly below the previous knot.

5. Slide a seed bead onto the holding cord and follow it with a square knot; leaving a small open space, next tie two square knots right next to one another. Leave another small space and tie one last square knot.

6. Repeat step 5; then slide one of the ¼-inch-diameter white beads onto the holding cord and follow it with three square knots close together. Braid the remaining lengths of the three cords (illustration B) until you have enough to tie around the wrist. Tie it in a knot, cut off excess cord, and dip the knot in white glue. Allow to dry.

7. For the other half of the bracelet, repeat steps 2 through 6, making sure both sides evenly match bead and knot placement.

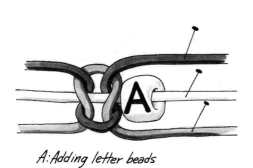

A: Adding letter beads

B: Braiding cord ends

Watch Strap Bracelet

(Color photo on page 44)

Watch strap bracelets are the perfect companions for any casual outfit, especially jeans and a sporty sweater. The bracelet described here uses a small reversible flat bead in place of an actual watch face, as well as a sequence of macramé knots including square knots, diagonal double half hitches, half square knots, and reverse double half hitches. For more macramé information, see page 19.

Equipment: A 12-inch by 12-inch square of composition board (Celotex), one box of T-pins or glass-headed pins, scissors, tape measure.

Materials: One ⅜-inch-diameter reversible flat bead with large hole; four strands of #18 maroon waxed nylon cord, each 3 yards in length; one ½-inch-diameter commercial metal watch buckle; clear-drying plastic-base glue.

How to Make

1. Fold all four strands in half to find their center points and mount them onto the tongue bar of the buckle, with two mounting knots on either side of the tongue (illustration A). Make sure the *back* of the buckle is facing you when you mount the cords. Pin the buckle to the working board to keep it from shifting around while you are knotting the bracelet.

2. Divide the eight strands into two groups of four cords each and knot one square knot in each group, using the center two cords as holding cords and the two outside cords as tying cords (see illustration B, below).

3. In the next row, leave the two outside cords at either side free and work *only* with the four center cords. Tie another square knot with the very center two cords as holding cords and the two remaining cords as tying cords (illustration C).

4. Repeat steps 2 and 3 until 28 rows or 1⅞ inches are completed (if your wrist is large, complete 2 inches of alternating square knot rows). End with a square knot tied with the four middle cords; then divide the eight individual strands into two separate groups of four strands each.

5. Hold the outside cord on the left side at a 45° angle pointing to the *lower right* and tie diagonal double half hitches with the three remaining cords (illustration D), using the diagonal cord as the holding cord. Tie two

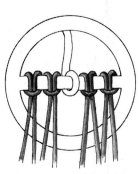

A: Mounting the cords

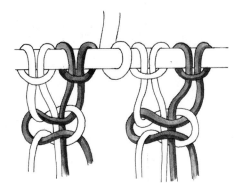

B: Tying square knots

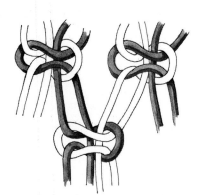

C: Making alternate square knots

D: Tying diagonal double half hitches

more rows in this manner, each time using the far outside cord as the holding cord.

6. Repeat step 5, using the remaining group of four cords on the right-hand side, but with the far right outside holding cord angled 45° to the *lower left* side of the bracelet.

7. Keeping the eight strands divided into two groups of four strands each, tie 14 half square knots in the left-hand group of four strands, using the center two cords as holding cords and the two outside cords as tying cords (illustration E). This will make a ½-inch spiral sinnet. Repeat for the remaining four cords, making a second ½-inch spiral sinnet.

8. Now regroup the eight cords into one group and separate the two center cords, leaving three cords free on either side. Pass the two center cords through the hole in the bead (if you have trouble, unwrap an inch on the ends of both cords, twist them tightly together, and coat the twist with beeswax). If only one cord will go through, hold the other one back and make it into a holding cord in the next step.

9. Working on the left side of the bead, use three of the six remaining strands to do a chain of seven reverse double half hitches (the exact number will depend on how many knots are needed to get around the bead), using the inside two cords as holding cords and the outside cord as a tying cord (illustration F). To form the tiny loops between these knots, space each knot a short distance away from the previous knot on the holding cord; then, when all seven knots are finished, push them all up tightly together. Repeat for the right-hand side of the bracelet.

10. When both sides are knotted far enough around to

meet the two cords holding the bead, again separate the eight cords into two groups of four and, starting with step 7, work backward through step 5, using the very *inside* cord in each group of four as the diagonal holding cord for steps 6 and 5 (illustration G).

11. Leaving the two outside cords on either side free, work *only* with the four center cords. Tie a square knot with the very center two cords as holding cords and the two remaining cords as tying cords (illustration C). Repeat steps 3 and 2 until you have 39 rows or 2½ inches completed. End with a square knot tied on the four center cords.

12. To make six final rows of diagonal double half hitches, three rows on the left and three rows on the right, start with the outside cord on the right side and hold it down *to the left* at a 45° angle. Use this as a holding cord and the remaining three cords as tying cords. When finished with that row, make the next row from the left angled down *to the right* at a 45° angle. Use the outside left cord as a holding cord and the three remaining cords as tying cords. When they have been tied, bring over the *holding* cord from the *first* diagonal row and use it to tie the last half hitch knot on the second diagonal holding cord (illustration H). Repeat this step two more times until you have three paired rows of diagonal double half hitches angling downward from the outside to the center.

13. Cut each of the eight cords to ¾ inch long, saturate them with glue, and fold them to the back of the bracelet. Glue them into place with more glue and hold them there until partially dry. Allow the bracelet to set overnight before wearing it. This will give the glue a chance to dry thoroughly.

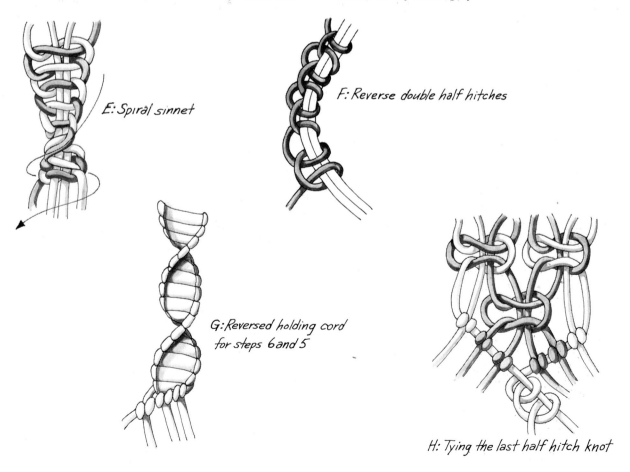

E: Spiral sinnet

F: Reverse double half hitches

G: Reversed holding cord for steps 6 and 5

H: Tying the last half hitch knot

Dainty Shell Bracelet

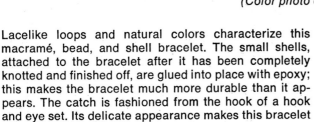

(Color photo on page 44)

Lacelike loops and natural colors characterize this macramé, bead, and shell bracelet. The small shells, attached to the bracelet after it has been completely knotted and finished off, are glued into place with epoxy; this makes the bracelet much more durable than it appears. The catch is fashioned from the hook of a hook and eye set. Its delicate appearance makes this bracelet a lighthearted companion for beach or evening wear.

Equipment: A 12-inch by 12-inch square of composition board (Celotex), one box of T-pins or glass-headed pins, scissors, tape measure.

Materials: One roll of 5-cord cocoa brown or canvas beige waxed linen, seven small brown or white seashells, seven ⅛-inch-diameter red or natural-colored wooden beads, white glue, epoxy, one hook (from hook and eye closures used for sewing).

How to Make

1. Measure wrist with tape measure and add two inches. Cut one length of waxed linen to this size. Then multiply this length by eight and cut a cord to the multiplied length.
2. Fold the long cord in half and pin it to the board; then tie a knot at one end of the short length of linen cord and pin it beneath the fold of the long cord, leaving a small space between them (illustration A).
3. Tie three square knots (see page 19), using the folded long length as tying cords and the short knotted center cord as a holding cord.
4. Next, tie three square knot picots (illustration B) by making one tight square knot, leaving a space, and then tying a second tight square knot. Leave another space equal to the first, tie a third square knot, leave an equal space, and tie one last square knot. Now push the bottom knot up the holding cord until all four square knots are close together. This will leave three pairs of loops on either side of the bracelet.
5. Tie two square knots; then slide a single bead onto the holding cord and up to meet the square knots.
6. Repeat the sequence from step 3 to step 5 six more times, tying one square knot to secure the last bead.
7. Slide the metal hook onto the two tying cords and tie two or more square knots to cover and hide the hook (illustration C).
8. Snip off all three cords and apply a dab of white glue to the ends of the cords. Allow them to dry.
9. Glue shells to the bracelet at points where the picot/square knot areas are located, using epoxy to give a firm bond (the shells will be stronger and less likely to break if they are filled with white glue and allowed to dry before being attached).

A: Starting the bracelet

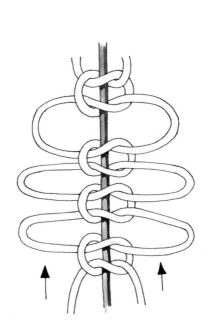

B: Square knot picots

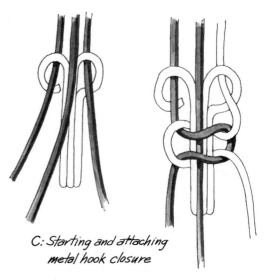

C: Starting and attaching metal hook closure

Seashells and Silver Bracelet

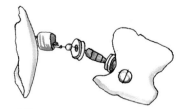

(Color photo on page 44)

A companion to the shell necklace described on page 25, this shell and bead bracelet looks like a chain of small white butterflies. Hand-rolled paper beads, clamshell hishi, abalone-shell beads, and round silver balls are all joined together with sterling silver wire for a very special effect. If you can't find the giant chiton (butterfly-shaped) shells, use small white clamshells instead, or add found objects of your own choosing.

Equipment: Roundnose pliers, wire cutters, hand drill and 1/8-inch drill bit, large blunt tapestry needle.

Materials: Five 1/4-inch-diameter sterling silver beads, seven 3/16-inch-diameter silver beads, two abalone-shell fragments (sold in hobby shops for mosaic table tops), two rectangular abalone-shell beads, 16 white clamshell hishi beads, two small seashells, two paper beads (see page 25, step 1), three large flat seashells (giant white chiton shells were used here), 18 inches of 24-gauge sterling silver wire, commercial bracelet clasp.

How to Make

1. Make two paper beads as explained on page 25, step 1; then set aside until needed.
2. Cut the 18-inch length of wire into three lengths of 6 inches each. Using one of the three lengths, make a loop at one end with roundnose pliers (illustration A).

Do the same for the other two lengths and set them both aside until needed.

3. On the first length, thread beads and shells in this order: one large silver bead, one abalone fragment (drill a hole in the piece before stringing), one small silver bead, two hishi, one small shell, two hishi, one small silver bead. At this point, drill a hole in the center of one of the large flat seashells and pass the wire through the hole until the shell and small silver beads are touching. Thread on a large silver bead; then pass the wire back down through the hole in the shell (illustration B). This holds the shell in place. Continue by adding one small silver bead. Make a loop at the end of the wire as at the beginning.

4. Repeat step 3 exactly, using the second length of wire, to make another link of beads and shells. Set both aside when finished.

5. For middle link, loop one end of the third length of wire through the *end* loop of the first link made (that one closest to the paper bead) and close it as in illustration A. Thread on one abalone-shell bead, pass the wire through a hole drilled in the large, flat seashell, and secure it with a small silver bead as in step 3. Pass the wire back down through the hole in the shell and thread on another abalone-shell bead. Loop the end of the wire through the end loop of the remaining bead and shell link and fasten it as in illustration A.

6. Add the commercial clasp to the bracelet ends.

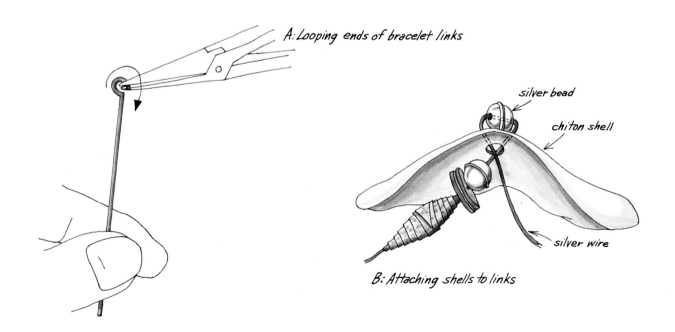

A: *Looping ends of bracelet links*

silver bead

chiton shell

silver wire

B: *Attaching shells to links*

Sea Shells and Silver Bracelet (page 43)

Butterfly-shaped sea shells join up with hand-rolled antique paper beads and silver beads in this charming offering from the sea. Design: Pat Deardorff.

Watch Strap Bracelet (page 40)

Macramé sunburst surrounds the flat bead "watch face" on this strap-and-buckle styled bracelet. Fine nylon cording is used for the band. Design: Luisita Amiguet.

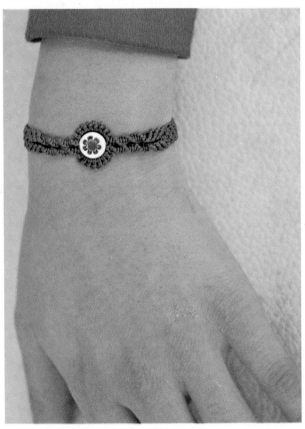

Dainty Shell Bracelets (page 42)

Delicate, lacelike macramé work provides a soft backing for tiny glued-on sea shells in graduating shades of cream and brown. Design: Tina Kauffman.

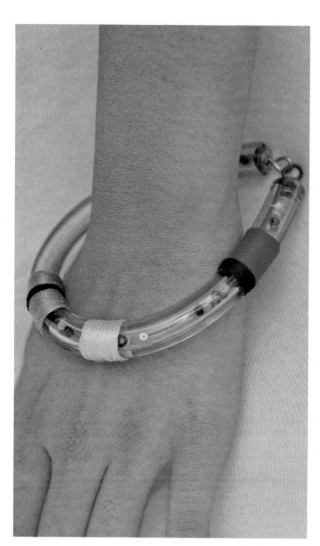

Beads and Brass Bracelet (page 47)

Black and white clam shell hishi beads team up with Indian seed beads and brass fishing swivels for an elegantly ethnic bracelet. Make this design into a choker by extending the length of the chain of shells, beads, and swivels. Design: Alyson Smith Gonsalves.

Plastic Flex Bracelet (page 46)

Clear, flexible plastic tubing can adapt easily to the role of bracelet, necklace, or belt. Pluglike, handmade hook ends form a secure closure for this hollow core plastic bracelet. Design: Alyson Smith Gonsalves.

Cufflinks by the Slice (page 48)

Handsome handmade accessories, these cufflinks owe their unusual appearance to softwood insets made from ordinary round toothpicks. Design: William Jacquith Evans.

Plastic Flex Bracelet

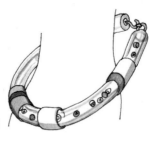

(Color photo on page 45)

Lending itself to lots of colorful interpretations, the plastic tubing bracelet can be wrapped with embroidery floss (as described here), painted with acrylic paint, filled with colored water and oil "layers" or small seed beads, and even threaded through with a multicolored bundle of flosses or yarns. The plastic tubing is available through plastics supply houses and some hardware stores. Check the Yellow Pages under "plastics."

Equipment: Art knife, roundnose pliers, wire cutters, scissors, toothpick.

Materials: 8¾ inches of flexible ½-inch-diameter clear plastic tubing, one package of Indian seed beads in assorted colors, one skein *each* of navy, red orange, lemon yellow, and lime green 6-strand embroidery floss, two ⅛-inch-diameter glass beads, two 1-inch lengths of 18-gauge copper wire, two ⁵⁄₁₆-inch #6 brass washers, jewelry cement.

How to Make

1. Force a small amount of jewelry cement into one open end of the plastic tubing and press one of the ⅛-inch-diameter glass beads into the glue-filled opening, clearing out any glue that may have clogged the bead hole.

2. Bend each 1-inch length of copper wire into a loop and stem (illustration A), leaving one loop slightly open. Thread one brass washer onto one of the copper wire loops and stems. Coat the stem and washer with glue and push them together into the opening in the ⅛-inch-diameter bead filling the glued end of the plastic tubing (illustration B). Allow the glue to dry until set. The copper wire loops will interlock to form the bracelet clasp.

3. Cut off lengths of floss from each skein of embroidery floss and wrap the tubing in this order: 1-inch tubing, ½-inch red orange, ⅛-inch navy, 1½-inches tubing, ½-inch yellow, ½-inch tubing, ½-inch lime, ⅛-inch navy, ¼-inch lime, 2⅜-inches tubing, ⅜-inch red orange, 1-inch tubing. To wrap the floss, wet one end thoroughly with glue and press it against the tubing until it holds; then untwist the floss and wrap it carefully around the tubing, laying the threads close together but not overlapping them (illustration C). End each strand as it was started, with jewelry cement. Continue until all colors are wrapped.

4. Put 50 to 100 seed beads inside the tubing, capping off the hole as in steps 1 and 2. Allow glue to dry for several days before wearing the bracelet.

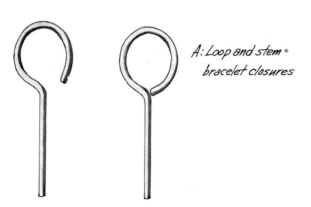

A: Loop and stem bracelet closures

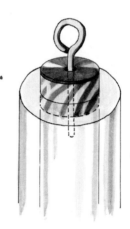

B: Plugging end of tube

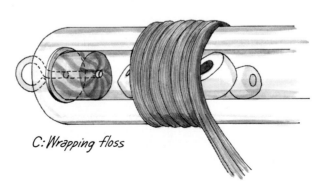

C: Wrapping floss

Beads and Brass Bracelet

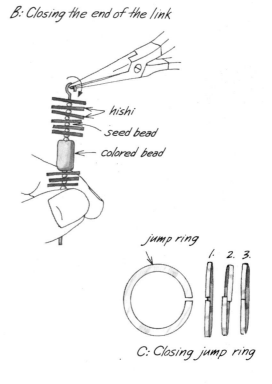

(Color photo on page 45)

Brass swivel links aren't just for attaching fishing lines to hooks and sinkers; here they're used to link together elements of a bead and clamshell hishi bracelet. The bracelet uses the method of multiple unit construction; that is, several links of the same design are joined together in a definite order to attain a special effect. The colors are varied between white, red, black, and brown.

Equipment: One pair roundnose pliers, one pair of wire cutters, one 3-inch length of ¼-inch wooden dowel, one table vise, one jeweler's saw (a scrolling saw with a fine blade may be used instead).

Materials: 24 black clamshell hishi beads, one package *each* of white and brown Indian seed beads, 12 white clamshell hishi beads, three ⅜-inch cylindrical red ceramic beads, three #8 brass barrel swivels (used on fishing lines), 20 inches of 20-gauge brass wire, one ¼-inch spring ring clasp.

How to Make

1. Make six brass wire jump rings in this way: horizontally clamp one end of the wooden dowel and one end of the brass wire firmly into the jaws of the vise. Wrap the wire around the dowel seven times, clipping off

remaining wire. With jeweler's saw, cut across the wire-wrapped dowel (see illustration A) to cut links apart.

2. Cut three lengths of wire, each 2¼ inches long. Holding one end of a length between thumb and forefinger, thread on hishi and seed beads in this order: one black hishi, one white seed bead; after repeating this five times, put on one more seed bead followed by one red ceramic bead. To finish the link, work backward, starting with two seed beads and ending with the sixth hishi bead. Grasp the free end of the wire at its tip with the roundnose pliers and bend it into a loop (illustration B). Do the same for the other end, trimming off any excess wire, as the beads should not run too loosely. Do the same with the other two sets of bead links, making one with black hishi and white seed beads, the other with white hishi and brown seed beads.

3. Lay the bead links, jump rings, and barrel swivels out in a row in this order: one ring, one link, one ring, one swivel, one ring, one link, one ring, one swivel, one ring, one link, one spring ring clasp. Using the pliers, bend the jump rings to open them and join the links and swivels in the order in which they were laid out. Make the jump rings close snugly by slightly overlapping their ends before using the pliers to bend them closed (illustration C). To make the bracelet fit the wrist more closely, bend each bead link into a slight curve.

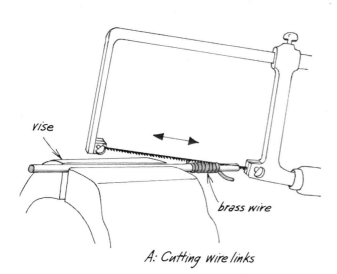

A: Cutting wire links

B: Closing the end of the link

hishi
seed bead
colored bead

jump ring

1. 2. 3.

C: Closing jump ring

Cufflinks by the Slice

(Color photo on page 45)

The secret of the elegant appearance of these walnut cufflinks lies in a box of common round cocktail toothpicks. Holes are drilled through a block of walnut; then round toothpicks are glued and inserted into the drilled holes. When the drilled block has been dried and sawed into slices, a gridlike polka-dot pattern appears on the face of each cufflink. To vary the grid design, drill the holes randomly or use colored toothpicks.

Equipment: Ruler, hand drill and ½2-inch drill bit, four grades of garnet sandpaper from 100 to 250, bench vise, scrolling saw, 3-inch C-clamp.

Materials: 1⅛-inch by 4-inch by ⅜-inch rectangle of hardwood (black walnut is used here), 16 round wooden cocktail toothpicks, multipurpose craft cement, 1 pair of commercial cufflink backs, wood lacquer (or oil or wax).

How to Make

1. Lay out a simple grid pattern on the wood as shown in illustration A. At each of the 16 points where the horizontal and vertical lines intersect, drill a hole with the 1/32-inch drill bit.

2. Squeeze craft cement into one hole and insert a cocktail toothpick until it fits snugly. Repeat for the remaining 15 drilled holes. Allow the glue to dry for at least 30 minutes; then break off the toothpick ends as closely

as possible on both sides of the wood piece.

3. When the glue has set, sand down both faces of the wood with successively finer sandpaper until it is smooth. For a very smooth sanded surface, dip the piece into water and allow it to dry before resanding with a fine-grit paper. Do this several times to achieve a highly refined surface.

4. Place the wood in a vise, and, with a coping saw, saw down the center of the wood as shown in illustration B. Don't saw completely through the length of wood; leave about an inch of wood uncut.

5. Clamp the sawed wood to the table or bench top with a C-clamp, leaving the sawed section projecting out from the table top (illustration C).

6. Draw the outline of the cufflink face on the upper surface of the wood (refer to illustration D for shape); then cut out both layers at once with a scrolling saw. Keep the blade on the waste side of the outline as you cut. When finished, you will have two matched pieces.

7. Sand off all rough spots; then round the corners and edges, following the procedure outlined in step 3.

8. When it is completely sanded to your satisfaction, clean the wood with a soft damp cloth and apply a wood finish such as lacquer, oil, or carnauba wood wax.

9. When the finish is completely dry, attach cufflink backings to wooden faces with jewelry cement. Remember to mount the backings on the wood so that the two faces are mirror images of each other instead of exact matches (illustration D).

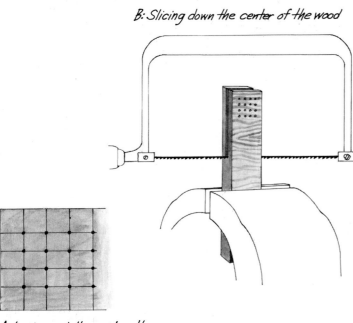

B: Slicing down the center of the wood

A: Laying out the grid pattern

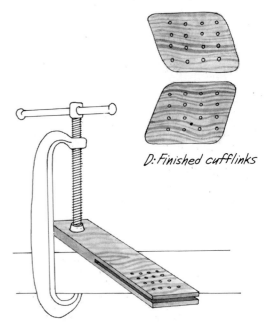

D: Finished cufflinks

C: Clamping the wood to the bench

Two-Tone Cufflinks

(Color photo on page 20)

Like the cufflinks on the facing page, these are simple in concept, yet visually unusual. A very large drill is used to channel an opening through a block of walnut into which a single glued wooden dowel is inserted. The oval appearance of the dowel on the finished cufflinks comes from cutting diagonal slices of wood to make the faces of the cufflinks. For a variation, drill more than one hole and use several glued dowels of different sizes.

Equipment: Hand drill and ⁵⁄₃₂-inch drill bit, four grades of garnet sandpaper from 100 to 250, table vise, miter box and saw, cotton-tipped ear swab.

Materials: ¾-inch by 3-inch by 1½-inch block of hardwood (black walnut is used here), one 3½-inch length of ¼-inch-diameter round wood dowel, multipurpose craft cement, one pair of commercial cufflink backs, wood lacquer (or oil or wax).

How to Make

1. Clamp the block of wood into a bench vise and drill a ⁵⁄₃₂-inch hole all the way through it, being sure to drill *across* the grain, not with the grain (illustration A), or the wood may split.

2. Swab the hole with craft cement, using the ear swab as an applicator. Also rub glue on the length of the dowel and insert it into the glued, drilled hole. Allow glue to set completely.

3. When the glue has dried, place the block of wood in a miter box and saw off two ³⁄₁₆-inch-thick slices of wood cut at a 45° angle (illustration B). Cut slowly to keep from splitting the wood grain.

4. Sand down all surfaces of each slice of wood with successively finer sandpaper until smooth. For a very smooth sanded surface, dip the piece in water; then allow it to dry before resanding with a fine grit paper. Do this several times to achieve a highly refined surface. Round off all corners and edges.

5. When it is smoothed to your satisfaction, clean the wood with a soft, damp cloth and apply a wood finish, such as lacquer, oil, or carnauba wood wax. Remove excess oil or wax with a damp soft cloth.

6. When the finish is completely dry, attach cufflink backings to backs of wooden pieces with jewelry cement, allowing them to dry overnight before wearing.

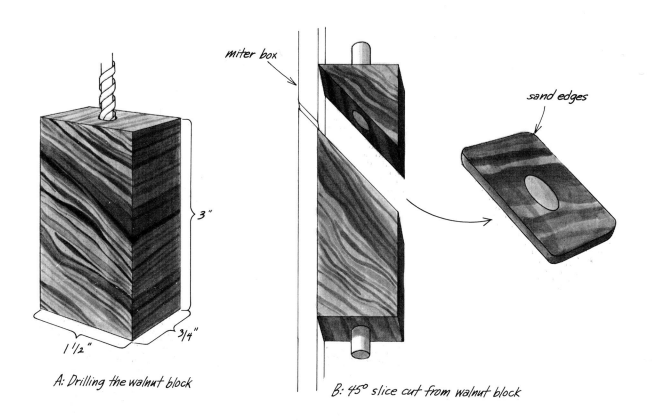

miter box

sand edges

A: Drilling the walnut block

3"

1½"

¾"

B: 45° slice cut from walnut block

Silver and Teak Inlaid Cufflinks

(Color photo on page 52)

A night on the town or a romantic dinner for two calls for a special effort to dress for the occasion. The perfect accessory to a silk evening shirt would be the understated elegance of these brushed silver and teak inlay cufflinks. The construction of the design calls for a sure hand and a degree of patience, as the working area of the cufflink is relatively small. If you prefer a polished finish, buff the face of the cufflink until it is glossy.

Equipment: Jeweler's saw, bench pin, compass, jeweler's equaling file, #150 sandpaper, small plastic ruler, pencil, tripoli, jeweler's rouge, scribing tool.

Materials: Two ¾-inch by ¾-inch squares of 26-gauge silver sheet, two ¾-inch by ¾-inch squares of 18-gauge brass (or copper) sheet, one 1-inch by 1-inch by 1/16-inch square of hardwood (teak is used here), jewelry cement, epoxy, one pair of silver-colored commercial cufflink backs.

How to Make

1. On each square of silver, scribe a circle ⅝ inch in diameter, using a compass with a large, sharp-pointed needle in place of the pencil lead. Do the same on each square of brass.

2. With a pencil and ruler, mark four lines across the face of each silver circle as shown in illustration A. Scribe the lines into the silver with the heavy needle used in the compass.

3. Cut out all four circles, going slowly to stay on the scribed lines. After they are cut out, file all edges to remove burrs and rough spots that may remain.

4. Cut apart the silver circles on the straight scribed lines, doing one circle at a time to avoid getting the pieces mixed up. File away any burrs from the outside curved pieces and center strips of silver.

5. To measure the wood pieces for faces of cufflinks, use silver sections flanking each center silver strip. Cut the wood pieces slightly longer on each end than necessary to fit the form of the cufflink faces (illustration B).

6. Coat the face of one brass circle with a thin layer of jewelry cement and, when it becomes tacky, press each piece of silver and wood into the glue in its proper order. Align all the edges, wipe away any excess glue, and set the face aside to dry overnight. Follow this same procedure for the second cufflink face.

7. When both faces have set completely, file the edges until the silver and wood fall flush with the edges of the brass backings. Polish the edges first with tripoli and then with red jeweler's rouge.

8. With #150 sandpaper, sand down the faces of the wood strips until they are flush with the surface of the silver. If you wish, polish each face with red jeweler's rouge and a soft rag; then give the silver surfaces a brushed matte look by lightly rubbing the sandpaper over them in one direction. Otherwise, the surface may be left shiny.

9. Apply a small amount of epoxy to the head of each cufflink backing. When tacky (which will happen quickly), attach the backings to the undersides of the cufflink faces. Stand the cufflinks on their faces and allow them to dry for several hours.

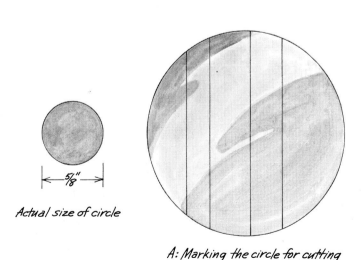

⅝"

Actual size of circle

A: Marking the circle for cutting

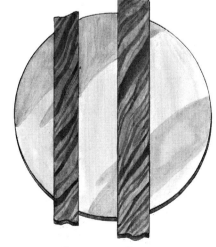

B: Inlaying the wood strips

Rough and Ready Leather Cufflinks

(Color photo on page 52)

The outdoorsman or naturalist will appreciate the casual good looks of this pair of wrap-styled leather cufflinks. Scrap latigo leather is cut to shape, then dampened and stamped with the carved, filed head of a 7-inch metal spike. When dry, the stamped design becomes a permanent decoration. For easier cutting and drilling, soften the metal head of the spike by first annealing it as explained on page 12, then by clamping its shaft into a bench vise.

Equipment: 7-inch metal spike, assorted jeweler's files, bench vise, hand drill, assorted drill bits, leather punch, art knife, table knife, heavy household hammer.

Materials: 5¼-inch by ¾-inch strip of 8-ounce latigo leather, white glue, one pair of commercial cufflink backings.

How to Make

1. Cut the leather strip into two lengths, each 2⅝ inches by ¾ inch. Round off one end of each cut strip. Cut off any uneven bits of rough leather on the flesh side (back) of the strip, leaving the grain side (front) and edges as smooth as possible.

2. Lay each strip along the edge of a table top and slide the blade of the table knife along the edges of the leather at a 45° angle (illustration A). This will bevel the edges and smooth them down. When you've finished, punch a ¼-inch hole as indicated on the pattern below and then enlarge it with one of the jeweler's files, as in-dicated. Set leather pieces aside until step 5.

3. Clamp the spike into the jaws of the bench vise with the head close to the top of the vise. With drill bits and files, cut a pattern into the head of the spike. To ease cutting, anneal the spike head first (see page 12), if you have access to a small butane torch. The design on the cufflinks shown on page 52 was made with a ⅛-inch drill bit, a jeweler's saw, and a triangular jeweler's file.

4. When the design has been cut deeply into the spike head, reposition the spike in the vise with the pointed end clamped into the jaws and the carved head and shaft of the spike lying *parallel* to the surface of the work table. With a jeweler's saw, cut off all but four inches of the spike shaft. File down any rough edges.

5. Pat the leather strips with a wet sponge to dampen the grain side; then place the wet leather on a cushioned surface (a piece of leather laid over a wood surface works well), grain side up. Place the head of the spike at the point where you wish the design to be, hold the spike firmly with one hand, and hammer the cut end of the spike two or three times with sharp blows, taking care not to let the spike head move about (illustration B). Repeat for second strip.

6. Allow the stamped leather to dry; then, on the back of each piece, place a generous amount of white glue at the rounded end of the leather and apply one cufflink backing; cover the backing head with more glue so that it is encased in glue. Repeat for the second cufflink and allow to dry overnight before using cufflinks.

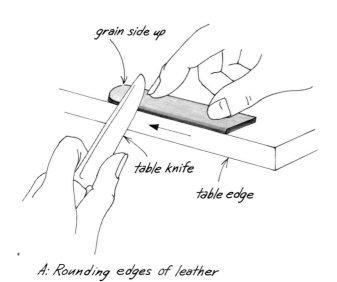

A: Rounding edges of leather

Pattern

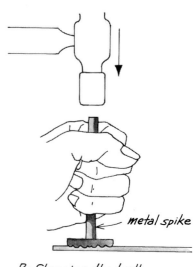

B: Stamping the leather

Two-Tone Cufflinks (page 49)

Walnut and pine woods make a distinctive pair of cufflinks. The center portion is a slice of white pine dowel. Design: William Jacquith Evans.

Silver and Teak Inlaid Cufflinks (page 50)

Wood grain against brushed silver gives an elegant appearance to this set of dress cufflinks created from teakwood and sterling silver. Design: Alyson Smith Gonsalves.

Rough and Ready Leather Cufflinks (page 51)

Butter-colored, latigo leather cufflinks are stamped with your own design and then colored with leather polish. For variation, leather dyes can be used. Design: Alyson Smith Gonsalves.

Fantasy Wrapped Yarn Pin (page 56)

Bright tassels and a soft, cuplike shape studded with wooden beads characterize this decorative yarn-wrapped basketlike pin. Design: Madge Copeland.

Tooled Copper Lapel Pin (page 55)

Put some art deco in your life: make yourself a tooled copper pin like the one pictured above. Use our design or one of your own invention. Design: Alyson Smith Gonsalves.

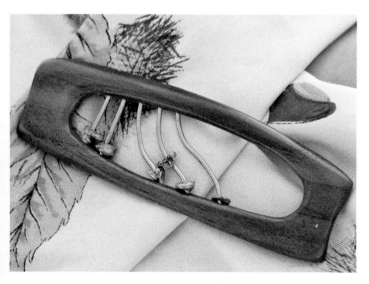

Walnut Scarf Brooch (page 54)

Softly rounded shape of this satin finish walnut scarf pin is set off by brass wire and bead decorative elements. Design: William Jacquith Evans.

Walnut Scarf Brooch

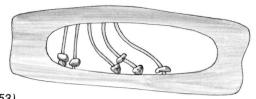

(Color photo on page 53)

Walnut and brass wire join forces to form a most distinctive shawl or shoulder pin, whose large size makes an ideal focal point for any number of outfits. Another possibility would be to convert the pin to a hair clasp by altering the position of the wires and by making a curved wooden "pin" slightly longer than the clasp to hold it securely in place at the nape of the neck. If brass beads are unavailable, use wooden ones instead.

Equipment: Scrolling saw or jigsaw, pocket knife, four grades of garnet sandpaper from 100 to 250, half-round file, hand drill and ¼-inch drill bit, #50 drill bit, wire cutters, roundnose pliers, carbon paper, pencil, soft cloth.

Materials: ½-inch by 1½-inch by 4¾-inch rectangle of hardwood (walnut, mahogany, or teak are good choices), ten inches of 16-gauge soft brass wire, seven brass beads (or others) with center holes large enough for the 16-gauge wire to pass through, jewelry cement, commercial pin backing, wood lacquer (or oil or wax).

How to Make

1. Make a tracing of the patterns below and transfer them to the surfaces of the wood with carbon paper and a pencil.

2. Saw out the basic shape with the scrolling saw or jigsaw, being careful to follow the patterns on the sides as well as on the front and back of the wood block. Carve the wood into a slightly curved profile with the pocket knife and file first of all; then rough out the basic face-on outline shape of the pin.

3. Inside of the oval area to be sawed out from the center of the pin, drill a ¼-inch hole with the hand drill. Cut out the inside oval with the scrolling or jigsaw by loosening the lower end of the saw blade, passing it

through the drilled hole, and refastening it. When you are finished, remove the saw blade in the same way as it was inserted.

4. With the pocket knife, half-round file, and sandpaper, round off the outside edges of the wood and the edges around the center oval. Give the surfaces of the pin a smooth, flowing quality with no abrupt changes or harsh edges.

5. Sand the final shape with successively finer grades of garnet sandpaper. For a very smooth sanded surface, dip the piece into water; then allow it to dry before resanding with a fine grit paper. Do this several times to achieve a highly refined surface.

6. As indicated in the illustration below, drill five holes in each long edge of the pin with a #50 drill bit, angling the holes in the direction in which the wire will go. Drill *very* carefully; clamping the pin on edge in a bench vise will help you to drill successfully (be sure the pin is protected with leather-covered vise jaws).

7. Place a little glue in the first hole at the top of the pin; then push one end of the 16-gauge brass wire through the glued hole into the open center of the pin. Put a bead on the wire; with pliers bend the wire into a graceful curve, and force the end through the corresponding hole (which should be glue-filled also) at the bottom edge. Clip off the wire with a wire cutter and file the wire down flush with the surface of the wood. Repeat for the other four wires, adding beads as you wish, passing the wires through the corresponding bottom holes, and clipping them off. File all wire ends.

8. Clean the sanded shape with a soft, damp cloth and apply a wood finish, such as lacquer, oil, or carnauba wood wax.

9. When the pin is finished and polished, glue the pin backing at the top of the pin's back side with jewelry cement. Allow it to dry.

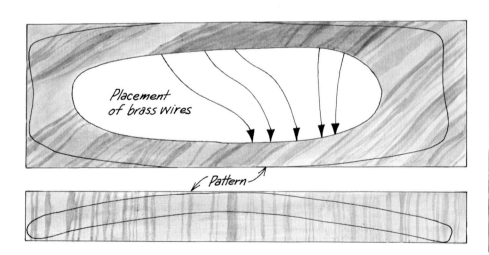

Placement of brass wires

Pattern

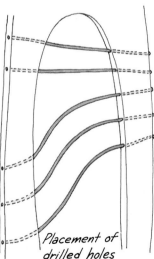

Placement of drilled holes

Tooled Copper Lapel Pin

(Color photo on page 53)

Give your lapel some flash with this bright, tooled copper pin. Its reflective surface and boldly engraved design are sure to catch the eye. The effect will be impressive, but the tools are simple: a ruler, an old ballpoint pen (one that is out of ink), and a small-diameter wooden dowel. From there on, the rest is up to you.

Equipment: One sheet of typewriter carbon paper, one sheet of tracing paper, masking tape, heavy duty household scissors or metal snips, 6-inch plastic ruler, scribing tool (hat pin, ice pick, old ballpoint pen, etc.), pencil, small-diameter wooden dowel, jeweler's rouge and soft rag, or copper scouring powder and steel wool.

Materials: Eight ounces of modeling clay, one 2½-inch by 1¾-inch rectangle of cardboard, one 2½-inch by 1¾-inch rectangle of copper tooling foil or heavy-duty aluminum kitchen foil, one 3-inch by 2¼-inch rectangle of copper tooling foil or heavy-duty aluminum kitchen foil, jewelry cement or epoxy, one commercial pin back.

How to Make

1. Soften and roll out the modeling clay like cookie dough to a size about 5 inches by 5 inches and about ⅛ inch thick. This will provide a firm but pliant ground on which to work the tooling foil.

2. Press the 3-inch by 2¼-inch rectangle of foil onto the clay until it is firmly held. Trace the design below onto tissue paper. Next, lay carbon paper face down over the clay-held foil and place the tissue paper design over the carbon. Tape into place with masking tape.

3. Lightly trace over the design with a sharp pencil to transfer it to the surface of the foil. When you are finished, remove the carbon paper, design tissue, and masking tape.

4. Using the ruler as necessary, tool the carbon lines into the copper with the scribe and wooden dowel. Take care not to puncture the foil while you are working.

5. When the design has been tooled, carefully pry the foil from the clay. Trim off the corners of the foil as shown in illustration A and trim all the edges to a ¼-inch width beyond the scribed outlines of the rectangle.

6. Place the tooled foil face down on the working surface and lay the cardboard rectangle over the back of the tooled foil to check for proper fit, trimming the edges of the cardboard if necessary. With the cardboard held in place, carefully bend the four sides, one at a time around the cardboard. For a tight fit, burnish the overlaps with the heel of a table knife to make them lie flat (see illustration B below).

7. With the pin on its face, lay the 2½-inch by 1¾-inch rectangle of foil over the cardboard to check for proper fit, trimming its edges if necessary.

8. When you are satisfied with the size of the backing foil, remove it and apply a small amount of jewelry cement, spreading it with a short scrap of cardboard to cover the cardboard backing and the foil overlaps. Position the foil backing and press it into place, carefully wiping off any excess glue with a soft rag.

9. Place the pin between two sheets of paper on a flat surface and cover with two or three heavy books. Allow it to dry overnight before gluing on the pin back, which should also be allowed to dry overnight.

10. Polish the pin by buffing it with red jeweler's rouge on a soft rag or with copper scouring powder and steel wool. Rinse and pat dry.

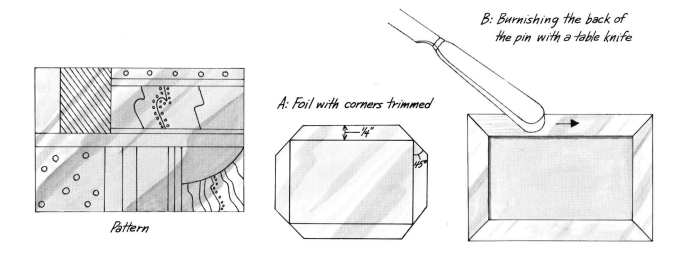

Pattern

A: Foil with corners trimmed

B: Burnishing the back of the pin with a table knife

Fantasy Wrapped Yarn Pin

(Color photo on page 53)

Impressive in just about every respect, this conversation piece in the form of a pin boasts bright, snappy colors and is put together on a scale which is sure to bring you comments and compliments. Knitting and novelty yarns wrap color around a core of plain clothesline, while small wooden and glass beads add sparkling accents.

Equipment: #13 blunt tapestry needle, scissors, ruler.

Materials: One 40-inch length and one 20-inch length of ¼-inch-diameter fiber clothesline, 13 yards of bright orange acrylic yarn, 10 yards red acrylic yarn, 6 yards hot pink acrylic yarn, 5 yards purple acrylic yarn, 10 yards gold acrylic yarn, 40 8-inch lengths of assorted yarn in the above colors, 12 wooden beads in related colors, 1 commercial pin back.

How to Make

1. Working from the back to the front of the pin, start with the 40-inch length of clothesline and wrap (illustration A) 7 inches of it with bright orange yarn. At this point, after wrapping 7 inches, attach the wrapped end to the rest of the wrapped clothesline forming a teardrop shape (illustration B).

2. From this point on, continue to wrap the orange yarn around the clothesline and to attach the wrapped line every ¾ inch or so to the teardrop shape as shown in illustration C. Continue to expand the teardrop shape

until you begin to approach the bottom of the third row of the teardrop.

3. To begin the second color of wrapping yarn (red), end the first wrapping color (orange) by laying the end of the new color along the clothesline and wrapping over it with the old color until three inches of the old color are left. Lay the old color along the clothesline and wrap over it with the new color (illustration D).

4. Attach the newly wrapped clothesline to the teardrop shape for approximately three inches; then move the clothesline around to the front of the teardrop as you wrap and form a complete circle with the teardrop shape as its support; continue to attach new wrapping to the previous coil every ¾ inch (see color photo on page 53).

5. Wrap and attach 3½ inches more of red yarn; then start to wrap on 2 inches of hot pink, allowing the pink portion to hang free. Trim off excess clothesline.

6. To add tassel fringe, use 16 8-inch lengths of various yarns in related colors and tie them all together into a bundle at their center points. Thread a tapestry needle with the yarn used to tie the bundle and then push the needle up into the wrapped clothesline. Pull the yarn through and clip it off. Repeat for the second yarn end.

7. To make a hot pink yarn bead, cut a 2-yard length of hot pink yarn and fold it in half. At a point ½ inch above the yarn tassel fringe, wrap the folded yarn around the clothesline several times to build up a bulky area of enlarged circumference. When it reaches 1¼ inch in diameter, cut off the excess yarn and tuck in the free ends

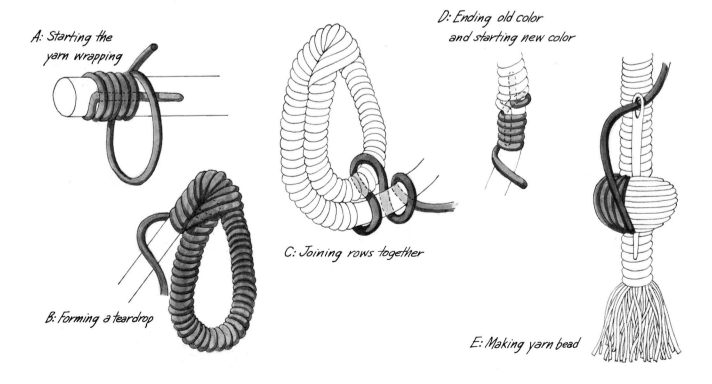

A: Starting the yarn wrapping

B: Forming a teardrop

C: Joining rows together

D: Ending old color and starting new color

E: Making yarn bead

to secure them. Thread one yard of hot pink yarn onto the tapestry needle and stitch around the thickly wrapped yarn as shown in illustration E. When you've finished, cut off the excess pink yarn; then wrap with gold yarn for ½ inch below the bead, ending as explained at the end of step 6.

8. Make a small tassel at the top of the pin (see photo) with four 8-inch lengths of yarn, attaching them to the wrapped area by threading them one by one under several wrapped threads and back out again, leaving them attached at their center points. Wrap all four together with orange yarn for ¼ inch; then thread all the ends through a large-holed bead.

9. To make the rest of the pin, use the 20-inch length

of clothesline and wrap a 1½-inch-diameter coil containing four rows of gold yarn-wrapped clothesline, attaching the rows as in illustration C. At the end of four rows, begin to attach the rows to the orange and red wrapped portion of the pin, setting the gold cylinder *inside of* the red wrapped area (see colored photo on page 53) and wrapping it with purple yarn. When one complete row of purple has been attached, wrap 3 unattached inches of clothesline with purple and push it through the cylinder to the front of the pin. Add tassels and yarn bead as in steps 6 and 7.

10. Randomly attach beads to all fringe and sew the commercial pin back to upper back area of the pin with orange yarn.

Pins of Paper

(Color photo on page 60)

Anything that has caught your fancy on the printed page can soon be worn on your sleeve or over your heart in the form of a paper pin. Backed with cardboard and protected with a plastic coating, this piece of jewelry can be cut from the glossy pages of magazines, trimmed from old-fashioned package stickers, or collaged from bits and pieces of your favorite printed matter. For a softer, more spongy feeling, mount the paper onto backings cut from styrofoam meat trays.

How to Make

Equipment: Wide-bristle brush, decoupage scissors (or use cuticle scissors or embroidery scissors).

Materials: One sheet of lightweight cardboard, one picture from a magazine or book printed on high-gloss paper, white glue, one can of clear polyurethane spray

paint, paint thinner, commercial pin back.

1. Cut roughly around the outside of the printed picture, saving close cutting work until later (illustration A).

2. Pour about an inch of white glue into a paper cup and dilute it by adding water until the glue has the consistency of thin cream. Stir until well mixed; then brush the thinned glue onto the back of the picture and onto the cardboard, covering an area slightly larger than the printed picture. Wait until both surfaces are tacky and then press them together. Wipe off excess glue with a damp rag and place the glued-down picture under a heavy weight. Allow it to dry overnight.

3. Trim off the excess cardboard from the picture (illustration B) with the decoupage scissors and then spray on two coats of clear polyurethane finish. Allow finish to dry; then coat the back of the pin.

4. When both sides are dry, attach the commercial pin back to the paper pin with white glue and allow it to dry overnight.

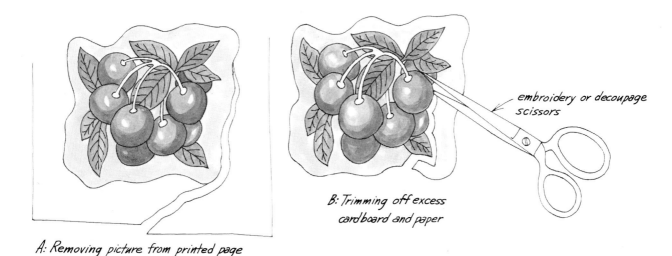

A: Removing picture from printed page

B: Trimming off excess cardboard and paper

embroidery or decoupage scissors

Hardwood Horses Belt Buckle

(Color photo on page 60)

Anyone with a sense of humor will appreciate this wooden belt buckle as a symbol of love, friendship, and mutual admiration. It could be made in several sizes, one to suit anybody from the smallest to the largest member of the family. Cut from a single block of hardwood, the buckle is then sanded into shape and oiled to a glowing finish. Any material can be used for a belt strap as long as its width doesn't exceed the width of the belt loops on the back of the buckle.

Equipment: Tracing paper, jig or scrolling saw, power disc sander (a sanding attachment for your power drill will work as well), hand or power drill, 1/8-inch drill bit, 3/16-inch drill bit, four grades of garnet sandpaper from 100 to 250, #00 steel wool, heavy-duty pliers, soft rag, jeweler's equaling file.

Materials: 3/4-inch by 4-inch by 5-inch rectangle of hardwood (walnut is used here), one 1/8-inch-diameter wooden dowel, two 4-inch lengths of 3/16-inch-diameter steel rod, rubber cement, epoxy glue, wood oil and soft cloth.

How to Make

1. Trace the design below onto the tracing paper and attach the paper with rubber cement to the surface of the wood block.

2. When the cement has dried, use the tissue paper pattern as a guide while you cut around the outside of the buckle with the jig or scrolling saw. Don't cut the two animals apart yet, but remove pattern and rubber cement.

3. Sand or cut the front and back faces of the buckle to make it curve to fit the contours of the body; that is,

cut the wood into a convex shape (illustration A).

4. When it's curved to your satisfaction, drill 1/8-inch-diameter holes for the eyes and gently tap in the 1/8-inch-diameter wooden dowels for the appearance of inlaid wood. Cut off any excess dowel flush with wood surface.

5. Sand down all surfaces of the buckle, rounding off all edges. Work from coarse to fine garnet paper. For a very smooth sanded surface, dip the piece into water and then allow it to dry before continuing to sand with a finer grit paper. Do this several times for a highly refined finish. Complete the sanding by using #00 steel wool.

6. Carefully cut apart the animals and saw their smiles out last. Sand all cut edges and surfaces as in step 5 until they are completely smooth. Finish with #00 steel wool.

7. Using a high-grade wood oil and a soft cloth, hand rub and buff the wood until the wood surface has a soft gloss.

8. File off both ends of each length of metal rod until they are flat; then bend them with the pliers as shown in illustration B. Position one rod on the back of each half of the buckle and mark the backs for drilling. Using a 3/16-inch drill bit, drill the four holes for the rods, fill the holes with epoxy glue, and insert the rods with the bends facing away from the center of the buckle. Allow the buckle to dry overnight.

9. To attach a belt, pass both ends of the leather (or fabric) belt length in the correct width between the bent rods and the buckle; then loop them back over the rods and out again. Adjust the belt length for fit and then attach fasteners (snaps or Velcro tabs) on the belt length overlaps at each side of the buckle.

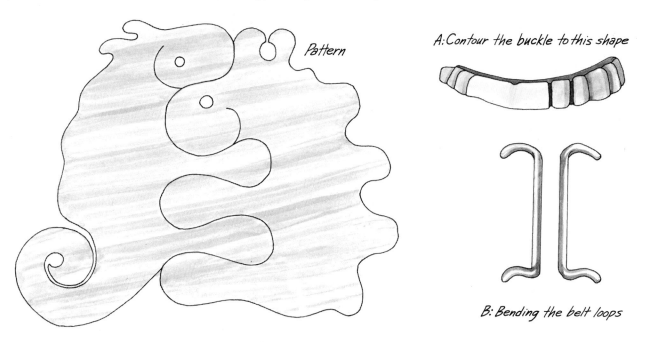

Pattern

A: Contour the buckle to this shape

B: Bending the belt loops

Silver and Turquoise Belt Buckle

(Color photo on page 60)

Here elegance takes the form of a silver and turquoise belt buckle. Cut from sheet silver and polished to a fine finish, this belt buckle is ingeniously constructed in a manner that holds the turquoise cabochon securely, yet requires no soldering. The prongs and belt pin are made by bending down several cut portions of the metal.

Equipment: Tracing paper, ballpoint pen, jeweler's saw, bench pin, one 3-inch C-clamp, assorted jeweler's files, 280 to 320 grit silicon carbide paper, 0/0 to 4/0 emery paper, buffing compound (jeweler's rouge) and soft cloth, hand or electric drill, 1/8-inch drill bit, heavy duty pliers, large nail, leather punch, hammer.

Materials: 1/8-inch by 1 7/8-inch by 2-inch rectangle of 10-gauge silver sheet metal (other metals may be substituted); one 7/8-inch, oval, flat-backed (cabochon-cut) semiprecious stone (turquoise is used here); rubber cement.

How to Make

1. Trace the design below onto the tracing paper, using the ballpoint pen. When you're finished, glue the tracing paper drawing onto the surface of the sheet silver with rubber cement and allow it to dry.

2. Using the 1/8-inch drill bit, drill holes through all the areas to be removed from the buckle design.

3. When all of the holes have been drilled, clamp the silver sheet onto the bench pin with the C-clamp, positioning one of the areas to be cut over the bench pin opening. As each area is cut out, reposition the silver over the bench pin opening to facilitate cutting out the remaining drilled areas.

4. Remove the lower end of the jeweler's saw blade and insert it through one of the drilled holes. Refasten the blade and cut out the area working slowly and carefully. The areas to be cut out will require frequent turn-

ing of the saw blade, so be prepared to cut slowly and to stop frequently. Angle the blade on some of the openings to make diagonal cuts exposing more silver in the cut-out areas (see photo on page 60).

5. Cut out each internal area, remembering to cut on the waste side of the design. Be especially careful when cutting around fingerlike prong projections.

6. When all areas are cut out, remove pattern and file off any rough areas or burrs. Then sand the surfaces with silicon carbide paper, working from 280 to 320 grit, and follow this with emery paper in successively finer grits. Finish the internal surfaces first with small jeweler's files and then with cloth-backed emery paper.

7. When polishing in general is completed, twist the finger prongs 90° from the plane of the buckle to form supports for the stone (illustration A). Do this with heavy-duty pliers, but first wrap the metal with cloth to protect the surface from being scarred by the jaws of the pliers. Bend the prongs slowly so as not to accidentally snap them off.

8. After they are bent, thin the prongs by cutting away excess metal with the jeweler's saw until each prong measures about 1/8 inch across. File and sand the cut prongs; then polish the entire buckle by applying red jeweler's rouge with a soft cloth or buffing wheel. Give all the exposed surfaces a good rubbing. For an easy way to make an electric buffer from your electric drill, see page 16.

9. To mount the cabochon stone, position it with four individual prongs below it and four above it (illustration B). Bend the lower prongs until the stone sits evenly on all four prongs. Then use a large nail wrapped with a soft cloth to bend the upper prongs around the stone. Cabochons are fragile, so don't force the prongs or use a hammer to bend them. Finally, bend the belt pin downward with the pliers.

10. Attach the leather belt to the buckle as shown in illustration C below.

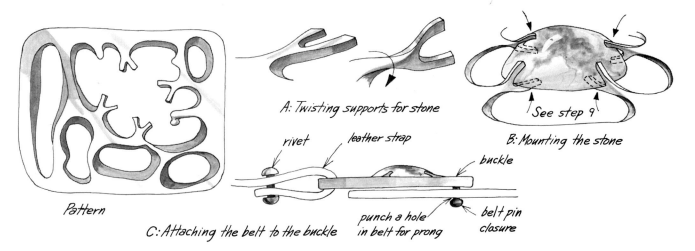

Pattern

A: Twisting supports for stone

See step 9

B: Mounting the stone

rivet   leather strap

buckle

C: Attaching the belt to the buckle   punch a hole in belt for prong   belt pin closure

Pins of Paper (page 57)

Any printed image can become a sassy little paper pin; just cut it out, back it with cardboard, and add a pin clasp. Design: Alyson Smith Gonsalves.

Hardwood Horses Belt Buckle (page 58)

Fantasy ponies play "huggy-bear" to form a clasp for this jigsaw-cut and hand-carved walnut hardwood belt buckle. Design: Vance and Polly Stanko.

Silver Belt Buckle (page 59)

Cleverly wrought prongs secure a cabochon of turquoise at the center of this cut-work silver belt buckle. Design: Charles DeCola.

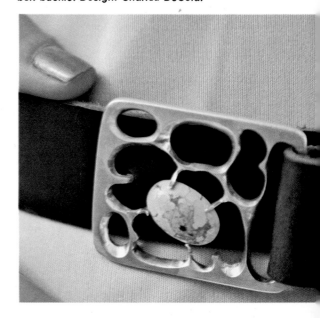

African Tribal Earrings (page 64)

Attractive dangle earrings in the spirit of Africa can be handmade easily with a minimum of tools. Add beads, shells, or other trinkets of your own choosing. Design: Leslie Correll.

Fringed Medallion Belt Buckle (page 62)

Body jewelry rather than a purely functional piece, this yarn-wrapped copper tubing belt buckle displays French coins dangling from wrapped fringes. Design: Nilda Duffek.

Teak and Copper Belt Buckle (page 63)

Classic buckle design characterizes this hardwood and copper sheet belt buckle. Brass wood screws act as decorative studs. Design: Alyson Smith Gonsalves.

Teak and Copper Belt Buckle

(Color photo on page 61)

Simple lines and classical styling make this teak, copper, and brass belt buckle a suitable accessory for any number of outfits. Both fabric and leather belt straps would work with this buckle, which uses small brass woodscrews as decorative studs. Fasten the belt with a hook and eye if it's made of fabric; otherwise set several grommets into the belt and attach a heavy-duty metal hook (easily purchased at a leather shop) to the tongue of the belt.

Equipment: Jeweler's saw; scrolling saw or jigsaw; jeweler's hand drill; 1/16-inch drill bit; #150, #100, and #80 sandpapers; 4-inch by 4-inch block of scrap wood; one 3-inch C-clamp; small screwdriver; jeweler's equaling and round files; tissue paper; carbon paper; pencil; scouring powder and soft cloth.

Materials: 3-inch by 3½-inch rectangle of hardwood (teak is used here), 2¾-inch by 3⅛-inch rectangle of 18-gauge copper sheet, fourteen #¼ x5 brass woodscrews, clear plastic spray or clear nail polish, wood paste wax.

How to Make

1. Copy the pattern below onto a piece of tracing paper; then transfer the design to the hardwood rectangle, with carbon paper. Drill holes into both center areas to be cut out. Then loosen the end of the scrolling or jigsaw blade farthest from the handle and pass it through one drilled hole; refasten the blade and cut out the area to be removed (illustration A). Repeat for the second area.

2. Sand all edges and both faces of the wood with successively finer sandpaper until you can't sand any finer. Then sponge the wood with water to rough up the surface. Allow it to dry, then sand it with fine sandpaper.

Repeat several times for a really smooth finish. Round off all corners and edges, rub paste wax into the wood, allow it to set for 30 minutes, and buff it to a soft finish.

3. Transfer the tissue design to the surface of the copper sheet, with carbon paper. Drill a hole into the center area, which is to be removed, and insert the blade of the jeweler's saw into the drilled hole as explained in step 1. Cut out the center of the copper rectangle.

4. When the rectangle has been cut out, file all edges until smooth, and round off the four outside corners. Polish the copper with scouring powder and a soft cloth; then coat it with a clear plastic spray or clear nail polish.

5. On the short sides of the rectangle, mark a pencil line down the exact center of each side and divide the side into eight equal sections (see pattern). Not counting both outside edges, this will give you seven division marks. Clamp the copper piece to a block of scrap wood with the C-clamp and drill seven holes along each side of the rectangle, using these marks as guides.

6. When you've finished, use the round file to clean off burrs pulled up by the drill bit. Then, in correct alignment, clamp the copper, wood backing, and scrap wood together. Using the holes drilled into the copper as guides, drill holes into the wooden part of the buckle, being careful not to go through the back of the wood.

7. With a small screwdriver, join the copper to the wooden backing by screwing fourteen #¼ x5 brass woodscrews into place. Give the brass screws a good buffing with a soft cloth.

8. To add a belt, rivet a length of soft leather, decorative trim, or belting, each approximately 2 inches in width, to the center post of the buckle (illustration B). To fasten the end of the belt, sew on snaps or hooks (for a fabric belt) or use grommets (for a leather belt). These can be purchased at sewing supply centers or at a leather supply shop.

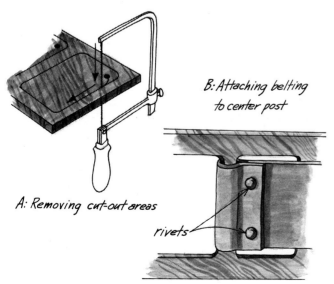

B: Attaching belting to center post

A: Removing cut-out areas

rivets

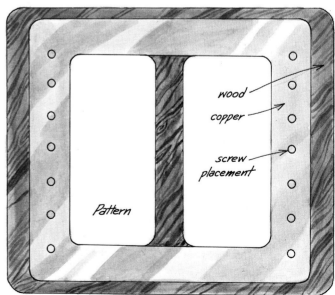

wood

copper

screw placement

Pattern

Fringed Medallion Belt Buckle

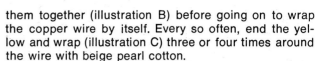

(Color photo on page 61)

Dramatic in appearance, the wrapped yarn belt buckle described below could be the focal point for an entire evening wear ensemble. Wear it slung low on the hips, for this buckle is meant to be a piece of body jewelry rather than a functional clothing accessory. Old French centime pieces drilled through and added to the cascade of wrapped fringe add an international flavor. If you haven't any old coins, use fare tokens or flat ceramic beads.

Equipment: Heavy-duty pliers, scissors, #13 blunt tapestry needle.

Materials: Three feet of #8 insulated copper wire (sometimes called TW wire), five skeins or balls of smooth-surfaced yarn in five different coordinated colors (used here are olive green worsted, lemon yellow linen, grey pearl cotton, beige pearl cotton, and black/silver metallic), 15 drilled metal coins (large-holed beads, charms, or other found objects can be used instead).

How to Make

1. Starting from the center and working outward, with heavy pliers bend one end of the insulated copper wire into a U-shaped loop approximately two inches deep.

2. With the lemon yellow linen, begin to wrap the bent wire until you've wrapped the entire U-shape with closely wrapped yarn (illustration A).

3. With pliers, bend the wire over and around the wrapped starting point into another oval slightly larger than the first. The ovals needn't touch at all points; as you work, allow the form to become slightly uneven in shape.

4. Continue to wrap with yellow, wrapping over both the continuous wire length *and* the starting point to join them together (illustration B) before going on to wrap the copper wire by itself. Every so often, end the yellow and wrap (illustration C) three or four times around the wire with beige pearl cotton.

5. As you progress, occasionally wrap over both the wire you are working and the previous bent and wrapped wire oval to hold them together (illustration D). About two-thirds of the way around, start to add segments of the other three colors in small amounts, keeping yellow as the main color.

6. When you've again reached the top of the oval, bend the wire again with the pliers until another concentric oval is formed. Continue to cover it with alternating areas of color, gradually decreasing the use of yellow and increasing the olive, brown, and metallic color range. Remember to wrap the outside oval to the inner ovals every so often to hold them all together until you near the end of the outside bent oval.

7. Bend the wire into a fourth concentric oval and continue to wrap with uneven alternating bands of color. Start to add areas of grey pearl cotton and yellow linen, attaching the outside oval to the previously worked ovals every so often.

8. Bend the final length of copper wire into a long oval with enough space at either end for a length of belting to be passed through. Wrap with long segments of each color, using grey, lemon, and olive as the predominant shades and black metallic as an accent.

9. With the olive green worsted, snugly wrap the end of the wire to the adjacent inside wrapped wire. To tuck in the end, thread it onto the tapestry needle and push the needle and thread back under the wrapping along the wire for two inches. Pull out the needle, using the pliers if necessary, and clip off any excess worsted yarn.

10. To attach the coin or bead fringe, cut a yard of each color to be used in the fringe and measure up seven

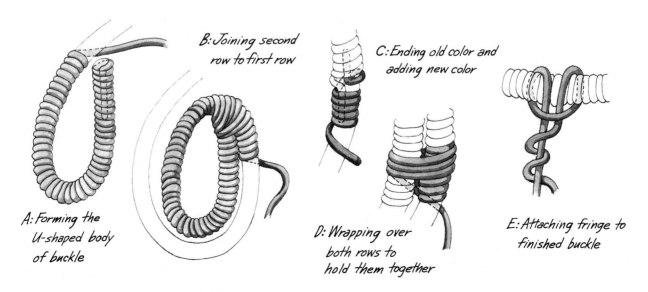

B: Joining second row to first row

C: Ending old color and adding new color

A: Forming the U-shaped body of buckle

D: Wrapping over both rows to hold them together

E: Attaching fringe to finished buckle

inches from one end of each length. Fold the yarns at that point and fasten them onto the bottom two rows of wrapped wire with a mounting knot (illustration E).

11. Hold the short length taut (tack it and the buckle down on a board if necessary) and wrap the long length around it from the buckle down to within two inches of the end. Thread on a coin or bead, fold back up the last inch of the short coin-carrying end, and wrap down over it with the long end.

12. To secure the wrapping, thread it onto the needle, pass it through the coin or bead, and push the needle and yarn end up the wrapped cord. Finish and trim off the end as in step 9. Repeat for all other ends.

13. To add a belt, use either a length of belting no wider than two inches, or a length of fine chain. Pass the ends through the large openings at either side of the outside oval and fasten with snaps or chain clasps to the insides of the belt ends.

African Tribal Earrings

(Color photo on page 61)

These copper disc and glass bead earrings are small but powerful eye-stoppers. Very easy to construct, they lend themselves to any number of variations.

Equipment: Roundnose pliers, household hammer, anvil (see page 12), hand drill, ½-inch drill bit, assorted jeweler's files, scribing tool.

Materials: 2½-inch by 1½-inch rectangle of 26-gauge brass or copper sheet metal, two small clamshell hishi or two flat pearl buttons, two flat trade beads or small seashells, two 1¼-inch lengths of dark annealed or brass 18-gauge wire, one pair of commercial earring backs or earwires.

How to Make

1. Trace twice around a 25¢ piece or paper pattern (measuring 1⅛ inches in diameter) which has been placed over sheet metal, transferring the outlines to the sheet metal with a scribing tool or pencil.

2. With metal snips or jeweler's file, cut out shapes; then forge the entire surface of the metal discs with a hammer and anvil. File away any rough edges for a more finished appearance.

3. Cut two lengths of 18-gauge wire, each 1¼ inches long. Bend one end of each wire into a tiny loop, using the very tip of the roundnose pliers. Flatten the loop with a few strokes of the hammer until it closes up tight and forms a metal "knot."

4. With pliers, bend this "head" back to form a "pin" (illustration A). Slip on one trade bead, one hishi or button, and one metal disc. Bend the wire up sharply behind metal disc at a right angle (illustration B) to hold the disc and beads; then twist the remaining end of wire to form a slightly open loop. Attach it to a commercial earwire or earring backing and close the loop with pliers. Bend the wire slowly to avoid breaking it.

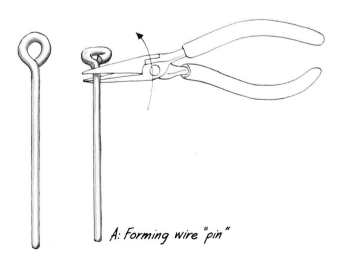

A: Forming wire "pin"

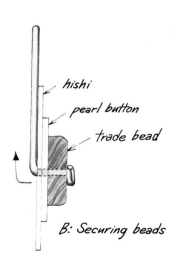

hishi
pearl button
trade bead

B: Securing beads

Celestial Moon Earrings

(Color photo on page 68)

Arcane symbols with a myriad of meanings and associations, the crescent moon and five-pointed star have been important signs to almost all cultures. What meanings do they hold for you? Ancient symbols such as these have evolved into good simple designs well suited to use in different forms of jewelry, like our sterling silver earrings. Cut them out, link them together, and create a "talisman" all your own.

Equipment: Jeweler's saw, bench pin, hand drill, $\frac{1}{16}$-inch drill bit, jeweler's equaling file (or carpenter's flat hand file), tracing paper, carbon paper, two pieces of scrap wood, one 3-inch C-clamp, bench vise, $\frac{5}{16}$-inch wooden dowel, roundnose pliers, 6-inch ruler, pencil, scribing tool, tripoli, jeweler's rouge, soft cloth.

Materials: Two 1½-inch by 1½-inch squares of 26-gauge sheet silver, 10 inches of 20-gauge silver wire, one pair of commercial earring clips or earwires in silver color (earwires should be white gold).

How to Make

1. Trace the design below onto a sheet of tracing paper. Next, put a piece of carbon paper over the surface of one of the squares of silver sheet and lay the design over the carbon paper. Trace it lightly onto the surface of the silver, indicating where holes will be drilled. Repeat for second square of silver sheet.

2. Remove the carbon paper and tracing paper; then scribe the design into the silver with a sharp pin.

3. Drill all the holes where indicated and carefully file off any burrs or rough edges from the holes. Try not to scratch the surface of the silver sheet, as the marks are very difficult to remove.

4. Brace the drilled square on the bench pin and cut out the half-moon and star shapes. Repeat for the second drilled square. File all the rough edges until they are completely smooth.

5. Polish out the scratches and shine the pieces by using a succession of polishing compounds applied with a soft rag, or by a buffing wheel (see page 16 for information on adapting an electric hand drill to this use). Start with tripoli; then clean the silver. Next, polish with jeweler's red rouge, again cleaning the silver when you're finished. Last, apply jeweler's white rouge to polish the silver to a high shine. To clean the small stars, place one point of a star between two pieces of scrap wood, clamping the wood tight (illustration A). This protects the silver and gives it support. Polish both sides of each star in this way.

6. To make jump rings, clamp one end of the $\frac{5}{16}$-inch wooden dowel and one end of the 20-gauge silver wire into the jaws of the vise. Wrap the wire around the dowel nine times and cut across the wrapped wires with a jeweler's saw (illustration B).

7. File the cut ends of the jump rings; then thread a star onto each ring. Attach the stars and rings to the crescent moon, using a roundnose plier to open and close the jump rings.

8. Attach the ear clips or wires to the single hole at the top of each crescent moon.

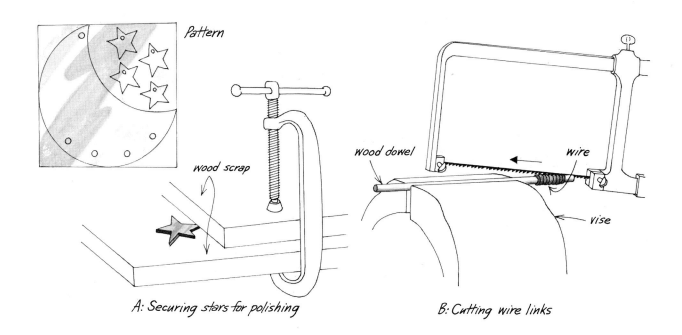

A: Securing stars for polishing

B: Cutting wire links

Tribal Totem Earrings

(Color photo on page 68)

Let these African-inspired, loop-style earrings with metal discs or coins reflect your good taste. Textural and visual interest is sparked by beads and unusual found objects. The procedure for making them is quick and simple, and the earrings are easily interchangeable with one another. The larger the loop, the more dramatic the earring.

Equipment: Roundnose pliers, household hammer, anvil (see page 12), hand drill, ½2-inch drill bit, assorted jeweler's files, scribing tool, wire cutter, large nail.

Materials: Spools of 16 and 18-gauge dark annealed or soft brass wire; assorted beads, coins, seeds, found objects; sheets of 24 or 26-gauge soft brass or copper sheet metal; pairs of earring backs or earwires.

How to Make

1. To make the basic earring: cut two lengths of wire, each 4½ inches long. Bend one end of each wire at a 45° angle to make a 1¼-inch-long stem (illustration A).

2. Using a small round form (cosmetics jar, lipstick tube, pill cylinder or bottle), bend the long portion of the wire around the form with your fingers, forcing the wires into a good round circle. Be sure to draw in the

end of the wire to make an even curve all around (illustration B). Hammer the curved end of the wire to broaden it and to finish off the end.

3. Slip a coin, metal disc, or found object onto the curved portion of wire (you may have to bend the wire to do this); then close the circle by overlapping the hammered end of the wire and the bent wire "elbow" (illustration C).

4. Add beads, shells, seeds, etc., to the stem of the earring and then finish the top by forging it into a large, flat teardrop-shaped end. With a large nail, center punch a mark into the center of the teardrop; then drill at the mark with a ½2-inch drill bit. File off all rough spots on the earring and add an earwire or earring backing.

To cut a disc and other metal shapes:

1. Trace around coins, small bottles, or anything else that will give you the desired shape, using a scribing tool or pencil.

2. With metal snips, cut out shapes; then forge the entire surface of the metal, using a hammer and anvil.

3. With a nail, center punch the point where the hole is desired, drill a hole with the hand drill, and correct the drill bit for the size of wire to pass through the hole. To drill coins, shells, and found objects, clamp them to a scrap of wood and use a hand drill to slowly put a hole through the object. File off all rough edges.

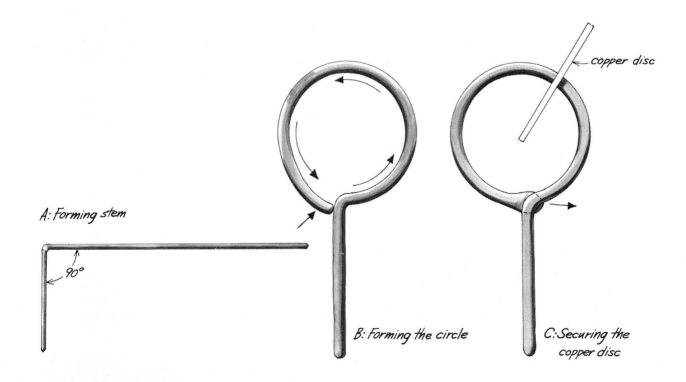

A: Forming stem

90°

B: Forming the circle

C: Securing the copper disc

copper disc

Mock Dresden Clay Earrings

(Color photo on page 68)

Though the effect is one of tinted porcelain, the material used to construct these earrings could be homemade kitchen clay or commercially packaged plastic clay. Color is added by kneading dry powdered fabric dyes into the clay before it's been formed or by painting the finished pieces with acrylic paints.

Equipment: Smooth glass or ceramic surface, art knife, two 3-inch by 3-inch blocks of smooth-surfaced scrap wood, one 4-inch length of ⅛-inch wooden dowel, one pair of rubber gloves, roundnose pliers.

Materials: One 3-inch-diameter ball of white play clay (use plastic clay or homemade clay as discussed on page 6), one package of magenta commercial powdered coldwater fabric dye, two commercial jump rings in silver color (or see page 65), one pair of screwback and dangle earring clips or earwires, one package brown Indian seed beads, two 1-inch lengths of silver or brass-colored 20-gauge wire.

How to Make

1. Divide the clay into three equal amounts, setting one third aside until later. Open the packet of powdered dye and shake out a small amount onto the glass surface. Wearing rubber gloves, knead the powdered dye into the remaining two thirds of the clay until they are thoroughly combined. Add a few drops of water to bring out the brilliance of the dye color; then set the clay aside for an hour or so to dry at room temperature.

2. Dividing the magenta clay into sixths, roll each out into a long clay "string" a little more than ⅛ inch in diameter. Make six 6-inch lengths of clay string. Set leftover magenta-colored clay aside.

3. Divide the 6-inch lengths into groups of three and make two braids as shown in illustration A. Set aside.

4. Rub a little cooking oil over the surfaces of the two blocks of scrap wood; then press the ball of white clay between the blocks until it is approximately ⅛-inch thick. Remove one block and then scribe two half circles into the clay. Cut out both pieces with the art knife and attach a length of braid to each curved edge as shown in illustration B.

5. Along the curved edges of the white clay, impress nine indentations with the end of the wooden dowel (lollipop sticks or birthday cake candles will work as well). Into each indentation, press one brown seed bead.

6. Make two ¼-inch-diameter balls of clay from the remaining magenta clay and press them flat between the oiled wood blocks. Lay one at the top center of each earring, pressing it into place with the decorative end of a piece of old silverware or a decorative bead (sealing wax stamps work as well).

7. With roundnose pliers, bend one end of each length of silver or brass-colored 20-gauge wire into a loop as shown in illustration C; then push it into the top of the earring.

8. Bake the earrings in a 325° oven for 20 minutes until the clay is hard. Use an old pie tin to hold the earrings.

9. When earrings are cool, thread them onto jump rings and connect each ring to one of the earring dangles or earwires.

A: Making braid trim

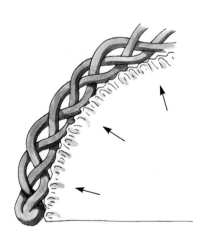

B: Attaching braid to earring

C: Making earring wires

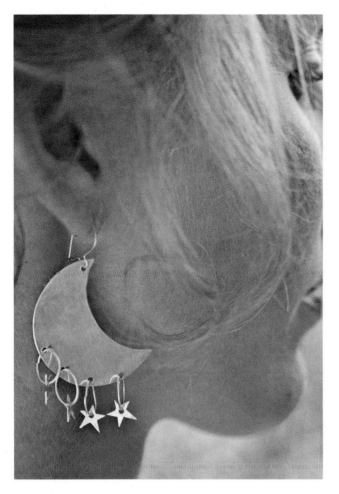

Mock Dresden Clay Earrings (page 67)

Soft pastel colors tint these procelain-like clay earrings. Powdered fabric dye provides the colors, and the texture is imparted by a braided clay rope trim. Design: Alyson Smith Gonsalves.

Celestial Moon Earrings (page 65)

Stars twinkle round these sterling silver crescent moon earrings. Their highly reflective surfaces flash and shimmer by sun or moonlight. Design: Alyson Smith Gonsalves.

Tribal Totem Earrings (page 66)

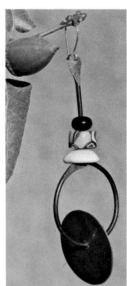
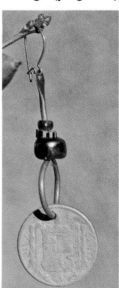

One-of-a-kind earrings of wire and assorted found objects (left to right): beads and abalone shell; corn kernel and hammered brass dangle; African beads and seashell; glass and shell beads with hammered copper disc dangle; assorted beads and drilled foreign coin dangle. Each of these earrings is made from the same basic design. Designs: Leslie Correll.

Bell Your Keys (page 73)

Ring bells with this idea: brass fishing swivels join a toy-size cowbell and a brass key guard to make a key chain. Design: Alyson Smith Gonsalves.

Gamesmanship Money Clip (page 70)

A miniature game as well as a functioning money clip, this silver and hardwood piece contains the nine individually functioning, three-sided modules of a tic-tac-toe game. As the game progresses, each module is turned from its plain side to a side showing a circle or a cross. Design: Charles DeCola.

Silver Status Key Ring (page 72)

Simplicity is the key to the good looks of this sterling silver wire and malachite stone dangle key ring. Overlapping ends of the ring open to add keys, yet close to keep keys in place. Design: Alyson Smith Gonsalves.

Gamesmanship Money Clip

(Color photo on page 69)

A real conversation piece, this attractive money clip sports a tic-tac-toe game with movable parts. The clip itself is sterling silver, while the game portion is made from silver-inlaid hardwood. Careful cutting and drilling are essential to the construction of this project.

Equipment: Tracing paper, ballpoint pen, jeweler's saw, scrolling or jigsaw, bench pin, one 3-inch C-clamp, assorted jeweler's files, 280 to 320 grit silicon carbide paper, 0/0 to 4/0 emery paper, buffing compound (jeweler's rouge) and soft cloth, hand or electric drill, 3/32-inch drill bit, #55 drill bit, #60 drill bit, 60° drafting triangle, center punch, hammer, electrician's tape, bench vise, scrap wood, nails.

Materials: 1¾-inch by 2¼-inch rectangle of 18-gauge silver sheet, one 3⅛-inch length of 3/32-inch-diameter silver tubing, 6½ inches of 18-gauge silver wire, 5/16-inch by 3-inch by 2-inch piece of hardwood (rosewood is used here), epoxy adhesive, rubber cement.

How to Make

1. Trace the designs below onto tracing paper, using the ballpoint pen. Remember to trace off two bar patterns, one for each spacer bar. When you've finished, glue the tracing paper drawing onto the surface of the sheet silver with rubber cement and allow it to set until completely dry.

2. Drill all the holes where they are indicated in the patterns, using the proper drill bits for each hole. Remember to drill slowly to avoid breaking the smaller bits.

3. Cut out each pattern piece, using the glued down tissues as cutting guides; then file and sand all cut edges until smooth. Start with silicon carbide paper, working from 280 to 320 grit, and finish the sanding with emery paper. Polish all the edges with jeweler's rouge applied and rubbed with a soft cloth.

4. When all the pieces have been finished, remove the tissue patterns and begin to bend the large sections of the clip into shape. Hold the money clip back (pattern B) in one hand and bend the tip of the cut-out tongue up until it curves to a point ¼ inch above the surface of the backing (illustration A). Set the backing aside.

5. To bend the framework for the upper clip (pattern A), cover the screw end of the C-clamp with electrician's tape, using it to clamp the framework to the corner of the workbench as shown in illustration B. Bend each arm down and back to point in the opposite direction from its original position (illustration C); then bend each arm into

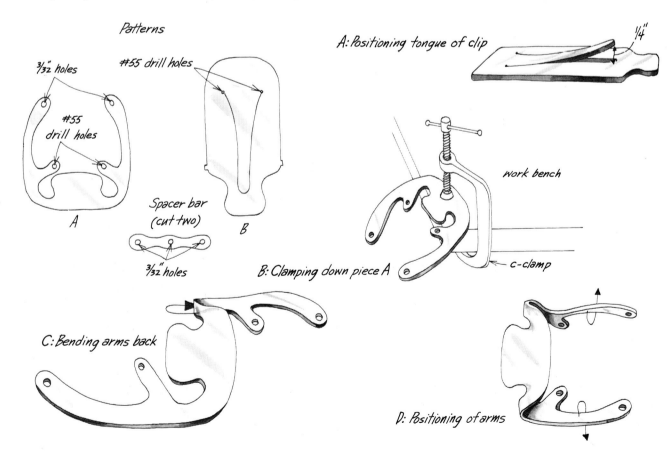

Patterns

3/32" holes
#55 drill holes
#55 drill holes

A

Spacer bar (cut two)
3/32" holes

B

A: Positioning tongue of clip
¼"

work bench

B: Clamping down piece A
c-clamp

C: Bending arms back

D: Positioning of arms

an upright position (illustration D).

6. To make the "O" and "X" modules for the tic-tac-toe game, first cut out a 60° equilateral triangular bar of hardwood measuring 3 inches in length and having sides each measuring 7/16 inch. To do this, use a 60° drafting triangle as a cutting guide, and with a scrolling or jigsaw, cut from the bottom edge of the wood, angling inward 60°. To make the second cut, measure 7/16 inch back from the lower edge and angle the cut to meet the top of the slope of the first cut (illustration E). To shape the triangular bar of wood to its final dimensions, sand each point of the triangle until the shape looks like that in illustration F. Sand all three sides of the triangular piece of wood until completely smooth.

7. To make individual modules, cut nine lengths of wood, each 1/4 inch long. Next, cut a small 60° triangle roughly the size of a single module from the edge of one piece of scrap wood. Then nail it and another piece of wood to a larger piece of wood to form a jig to hold each module while it is being drilled (illustration G). Drill a 3/32-inch hole through the center of each module, using light pressure to prevent the wood from splitting.

8. Inlay the silver designs by drilling shallow (less than 1/16 inch) holes in an "O" pattern on one side of each module and in an "X" pattern on the second side of each module, leaving the third side blank. When all the holes have been drilled, dip the end of the length of 18-gauge silver wire into epoxy and insert it into one of the holes. Cut the wire with a jeweler's saw close to the face of the wood. Dip the end into epoxy again and repeat this step until all the holes are inlaid with silver wire. When they're dry, file the silver level with the face of the wood.

9. Give the modules a final sanding; then rub mineral oil or wood oil into the wood and allow it to set for a half hour, removing any excess oil with a clean rag.

10. Cut the length of silver tubing into two lengths of 1 inch each and one length of 1 1/8 inch. Thread three modules onto each length of tubing, making sure that the "O"s and "X"s line up properly.

11. To attach the rows of modules to the spacer bars, fit the three tubes into the three holes of one of the spacers. Repeat for the second spacer bar; you will have one spacer bar on each side of the rows of modules. The tubes should extend out about 1/16 inch on either side of the spacer bars. Place a small piece of heavy paper from a matchbook cover between the wood and the spacer bars to protect their surfaces. Then stand the entire piece on its side and use the center punch and hammer to flare the ends of the two *outside* tubes. *Leave the longer center tube unattached.* To flare the tubes, place the tip of the punch inside the tube end and hammer with light blows on the punch. This will spread the tube end and hold the tube and modules in place on the spacer bars (illustration H). To flatten the flare, hammer *very* lightly directly on the flare until it is flat. Repeat until both *outside* tubes are flared at both ends and thus attached to the spacer bars. Set aside until step 13.

12. To attach the two main pieces of the money clip to one another, take pattern piece A and bend the lower drilled prongs until they are 7/8 inch apart (illustration I). Then lay pattern piece A on its face and place pattern piece B over piece A with the bent tongue pointing downward. Slip the two small pegs at each side of pattern piece B into the drilled prongs of pattern piece A (illustration J).

13. Add the tic-tac-toe portion to pattern piece A by passing the ends of the center tube through the drilled holes in both long arms of pattern piece A. As in step 11, flare and flatten the tube ends to join the pieces.

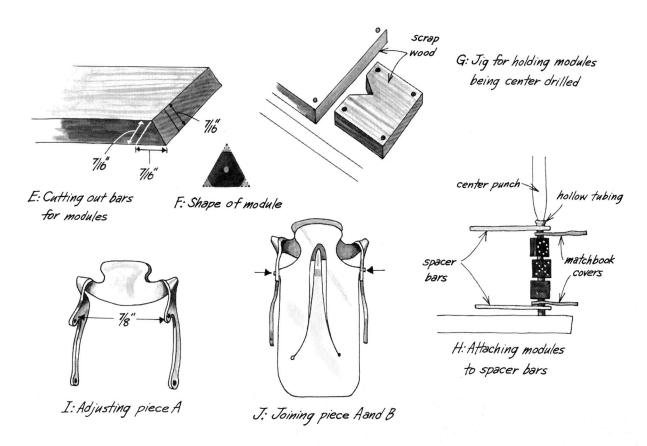

E: Cutting out bars for modules

F: Shape of module

G: Jig for holding modules being center drilled

H: Attaching modules to spacer bars

I: Adjusting piece A

J: Joining piece A and B

Silver Status Key Ring

(Color photo on page 69)

Simplicity equals elegance when silver is combined with semiprecious stone; such is the case with this well-bred malachite and sterling wire key ring. Just part the overlapping wires and slide on your keys — they'll never run the risk of being individually lost or misplaced.

Equipment: Jeweler's saw, equaling needle file or carpenter's flat hand file with fine teeth, 4-inch length of ¼-inch-diameter wooden dowel, two pairs of roundnose jeweler's pliers, short length of ⅞-inch-diameter wooden dowel or metal pipe (for forming key ring).

Materials: 4-inch length of 14-gauge square silver wire (round wire can be substituted), 3 inches of 20-gauge silver wire, one semiprecious stone bead ½ inch in diameter and center-drilled.

How to Make

1. Clamp the length of metal pipe or tubing into the jaws of the vise. File both ends of the square wire until they are flat (illustration A), then bend the wire around the pipe, overlapping the excess wire (illustration B).

2. If the wire doesn't lie properly on the overlap, move one overlapping length to the other side of the other overlapping length (illustration C). Make further adjustments with roundnose pliers, being careful not to mar the surface of the metal.

3. Remove the length of pipe from the vise and insert the ¼-inch wooden dowel and one end of the 3-inch length of 20-gauge silver wire. Clamp them in tight and wrap the wire around the dowel two times. Reposition the wire-wrapped dowel as shown in illustration D and cut across the wrapped wire with a jeweler's saw to separate the jump rings. Set the rings aside.

4. Pass the remaining length of 20 gauge wire through the bead and grasp the free end of the wire with roundnose pliers. Bend it into a circle. One-quarter inch up from the top of the bead, make another loop and wrap the remaining wire around the bead stem going toward the bead. Tuck the free end into the hole in the bead.

5. Attach the bead to large square-wire ring with a silver jump ring, using roundnose pliers to close the jump ring.

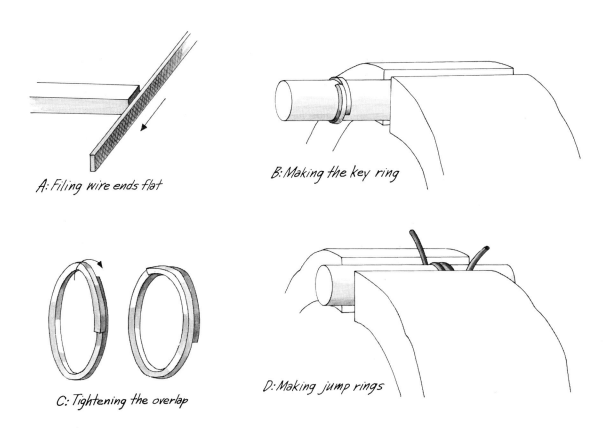

A: Filing wire ends flat

B: Making the key ring

C: Tightening the overlap

D: Making jump rings

Bell Your Keys

(Color photo on page 69)

Have you ever had trouble locating your keys? It will never happen again if you string them onto this key chain. A lively bell dangles from one end, a flat C-shaped curve from the other. Just thread the keys over the C-shaped curve and onto the chain; the jingling bell will guide you to them if they're lost in the depths of your purse, bikebag, or briefcase.

Equipment: Jeweler's saw, compass, hand drill, ⅟₁₆-inch drill bit, bench pin (see page 12), half-round needle file (or a carpenter's small 10-inch round file), pencil, ¼-inch wooden dowel, bench vise, wire cutters, two pairs of roundnose pliers, four inches of 12-gauge wire (for forming jump rings).

Materials: 1-inch by 1-inch square of 16-gauge brass sheet metal, five inches of 20-gauge brass wire, six #12 brass swivels, one small metal bell.

How to Make

1. Clamp part of the 4-inch length of 12-gauge wire and one end of the 5-inch length of 20-gauge brass wire into the jaws of the bench vise. As in the bracelet project on page 47, wrap the 20-gauge wire around the 12-gauge wire six times; then cut across the wrapped wire with a jeweler's saw to cut apart individual jump rings.

2. Join the six #12 brass swivels with the jump rings, using both pairs of roundnose pliers to close the rings.

3. As in step 1, make two brass jump rings using a ¼-inch wooden dowel rather than 12-gauge wire for the wrapping support. Cut the rings apart and set them

aside until they are needed for step 9.

4. Clean the brass sheet with a paste of scouring powder, rubbing in different directions with steel wool to avoid scarring the surface of the metal.

5. Replace the lead in your compass with a sharp-pointed tip, such as a large sewing needle, and scribe two concentric circles, ⅛-inch apart, on the surface of the 1-inch by 1-inch square of brass. With a pencil, mark the circle off into thirds, scribe two of the marks into the metal, and erase the third (illustration A).

6. Brace the marked brass square on the bench pin and saw out the partial circle, going slowly to keep the saw cuts accurate along the curved lines.

7. When you've finished, clamp the rough-cut semicircle into the vise and file off all rough edges with the round file.

8. Remove the semicircle from the vise, and, finding the halfway point on the semicircle, mark it with a pencil (illustration B). With a ⅟₁₆-inch drill bit, use a hand drill to drill a hole at the pencil mark. File the edges of the hole until they're smooth and finished.

9. Join the finished semicircle to the chain of brass swivels with one of the large jump rings made in step 3. Lightly hammer the ring until it is oval instead of round.

10. Add the bell to the other end of the brass swivel chain with another large jump ring from step 3. Use roundnose pliers to work the rings.

11. To string keys, slip one end of the semicircle through the key eye and slide the key along the semicircle, over the brass swivels and off the other end of the semicircle onto the swivel chain (illustration C). To remove keys, reverse this step.

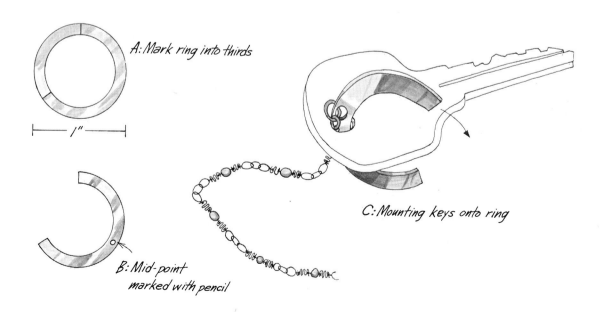

A: Mark ring into thirds

1"

B: Mid-point marked with pencil

C: Mounting keys onto ring

Rainbow's End Leather Key Ring

(Color photo on page 76)

If you appreciate casual accessories with honest faces and little pretense, this painted leather key ring will suit your taste. A cheerful design has been cut into the leather, painted with bright colors, and sprayed with a clear plastic coating to prevent chips and cracks. Simple, durable construction means that you can make this key ring quickly and use it for as long as you wish.

Equipment: Swivel knife (see page 35), art knife, ruler, pencil, ballpoint pen, tracing paper, wool dauber, #00 camel's hair brush, toothpick, leather punch or hand drill, and 1/8-inch drill bit.

Materials: 2-inch by 4-inch rectangle of 6 or 8-ounce latigo leather; one bottle *each* of acrylic-base red, yellow, blue, green, brown, white, and black leather paints; clear plastic spray; 1¼-inch commercial brass key ring or notebook ring.

How to Make

1. Copy one of the patterns below onto tracing paper; then dampen the surface of the leather rectangle with a sponge and transfer the design to the leather by going over the tracing with a ballpoint pen. Following the traced outlines, cut out the leather rectangle with the art knife and ruler, rounding off all four corners in the process. At one end of the rectangle, punch or drill a 1/8-inch hole through the leather.

2. Now use the swivel knife to cut the traced design into the leather. If you aren't sure how to use a swivel knife, practice first on a piece of scrap leather (see the illustration below showing how to use one).

3. With a piece of lamb's wool, daub a water-thinned but even coat of the background color over the entire piece, both front and back. Allow it to dry for an hour or more. A second coat may be necessary to completely color the leather. Again, allow an hour or more of drying time before proceeding.

4. To apply the actual design, use a #00 camel's hair brush and full strength paint. Two or three coats may be necessary to cover a dark background. If so, allow the paint to dry thoroughly between applications. When the leather is completely dry, spray on a protective coating of clear plastic to prevent moisture and chipping from damaging your design.

5. When the paints and spray coating are completely dry, pass the leather dangle onto the brass key or notebook ring.

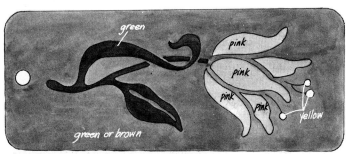

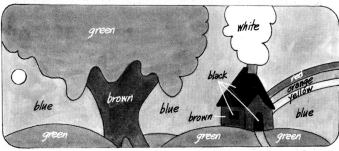

Patterns

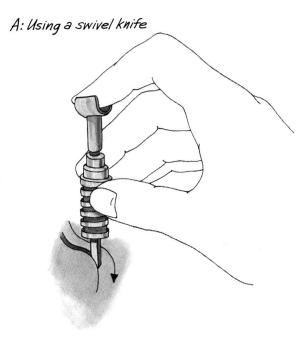

A: Using a swivel knife

Sculptural Fiber Key Ring

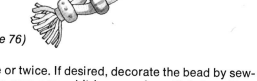

(Color photo on page 76)

For bright good looks and sheer frivolity, especially if you have a large purse or handbag, this fiber-wrapped key ring can't be beat. Of if you keep household keys on a board by the kitchen door, how about making different colored fiber dangles in varying lengths as guides to each key's use? It would make for an unusually interesting wall decoration.

Equipment: #13 blunt tapestry needle, scissors, ruler.

Materials: Forty 1½-yard-long strands of wool yarn in grape, magenta, cherry, hot pink, light pink, and orange (use odds and ends, preferably of varying thicknesses); one commercial brass key ring or notebook binder ring; 1½ feet of ⅛-inch-diameter fiber clothesline.

How to Make

1. Holding the 40 strands of yarn so that all are even, pull all strands through the ring until 31 inches hang on one side of the ring and 9 inches on the other. The 9-inch lengths form the basic core of the keyring dangle; the 31-inch lengths are used for wrapping.

2. Wrap one 31-inch length of cherry-colored yarn tightly around *all* other yarns and continue to wrap downward until you have gone ½ inch. Using a tapestry needle, thread the remaining length back into the working yarns to secure the wrapping.

3. To make a yarn bead, wrap three of the thickest yarn lengths horizontally around *all* the yarn lengths just below the cherry yarn wrapped area until you have a ball about two inches in diameter. Wrap the yarns firmly but not too tightly. Thread the tapestry needle with one 31-inch, grape-colored length of yarn, and, with the needle point *always down,* sew the yarn around the horizontally wrapped area (see illustration A) until it is completely covered. Anchor the yarn by sewing through the

core once or twice. If desired, decorate the bead by sewing orange yarn around it in a running stitch (see illustration B).

4. As in step 2, wrap light pink yarn for ½ inch around *all* lengths; then attach one end of the 1½-foot length of clothesline by wrapping over ¼ inch of it with the light pink yarn. Secure the wrapping yarn.

5. Wrap the clothesline with a 31-inch length of orange yarn and, as you wrap, work the clothesline around the core into three rows, attaching the second and third rows to the rows ahead of them as shown in illustration C. Hide the end of the clothesline by wrapping it together with all other yarns, using a 31-inch length of hot pink yarn and wrapping it for ¼ inch.

6. Separate the yarns into two equal groups and wrap the one on the left for 1½ inches with cherry yarn. Then make a 1½-inch-diameter yarn bead as in step 3, using light pink yarns for the horizontal wrapping and grape and orange yarns for the vertical wrapping. Finish the length by wrapping for one inch with hot pink yarn.

7. Wrap the second group of yarns for one inch with light pink yarn and make a 1½-inch-diameter yarn bead using three heavy yarns for the horizontal wrapping and grape yarn for the vertical wrapping. Finish by wrapping for 1½ inches with cherry yarn.

8. Use the remaining cherry yarn to wrap both beaded lengths back together. Secure the yarn by running it back up into the core with a tapestry needle. Clip off excess.

9. Make one last yarn bead, two inches in diameter, using grape yarn for the horizontal wrap and hot pink for the vertical wrap. If you like, make French knots around the yarn bead with grape yarn (illustration D).

10. Wrap all lengths together for ½ inch with orange yarn, secure the end, and cut off the remaining tassels to 1½ inches in length.

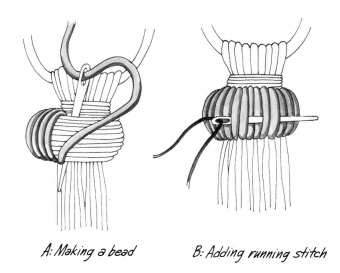

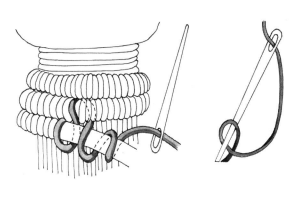

A: Making a bead   *B: Adding running stitch*   *C: Joining rows*   *D: French knot*

Sculptural Fiber Key Ring (page 75)

Bright, boldly colored yarns wrap up a really distinctive key ring. Yarn "beads" are made by vertically wrapping a horizontally wound yarn core until a solid bead is formed. Design: Madge Copeland.

Rainbow's End
Leather Key Ring (page 74)

Painted leather makes a picture-pretty key ring in two styles: the sparkling bright country scene shown here and a delicate art nouveau floral design found on page 74. Design: Shirley Pilkington.

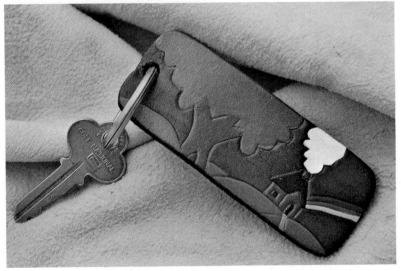

Two Silver Rings (page 78)

Delicate cut-work on heavy gauge silver sheet produced this amusing finger ring. Actual size of the ring shown is approximately ¾ of an inch across. Design: Charles DeCola.

Beads and Clay Ring (page 79)

Plastic clay ring is flexible when finished but sturdy and lightweight enough to be worn always. Powdered fabric dyes and seed beads provide color. Design: Alyson Smith Gonsalves.

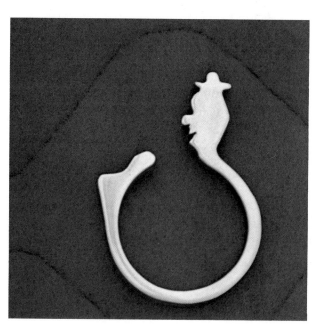

Two Silver Rings (page 78)

Almost foot-in-mouth, our clown ring is cut from heavy gauge silver sheet but can be adjusted easily to fit a number of finger sizes. Design: Charles DeCola.

Two Silver Rings

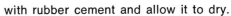

(Color photo on page 77)

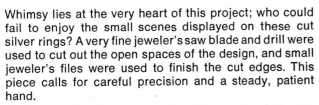

Whimsy lies at the very heart of this project; who could fail to enjoy the small scenes displayed on these cut silver rings? A very fine jeweler's saw blade and drill were used to cut out the open spaces of the design, and small jeweler's files were used to finish the cut edges. This piece calls for careful precision and a steady, patient hand.

Equipment: Tracing paper, ballpoint pen, jeweler's saw with 2/0 blade, bench pin, one 3-inch C-clamp, assorted jeweler's files, 280 to 320 grit silicon carbide paper, 0/0 to 4/0 emery paper, buffing compound (red jeweler's rouge) and soft cloth, a short length of wooden dowel slightly smaller in diameter than the finger opening of the ring, hand or electric drill, #60 to #65 small twist drills, medium-sized nail and household hammer, compass.

Materials: 1-inch by 1¼-inch by ⅛-inch rectangle of 10-gauge silver sheet metal (other metals may be substituted), rubber cement.

How to Make

1. Determine the correct ring size by measuring a ring that already fits correctly or by cutting a strip of paper, fitting it onto the finger (not too tightly), and marking the overlaps on the strip (illustration A).

2. With a compass, draw a circle of the correct ring size onto the tracing paper; then draw another circle around and ⅟₃₂ inch outside of the first circle to make the ring band.

3. Next, trace one of the designs below (or your own design) onto the edge of the tracing paper ring pattern, using a ballpoint pen. When you've finished, glue the tracing paper drawing onto the surface of the sheet silver with rubber cement and allow it to dry.

4. Mark all the areas to be cut away from design by tapping the tip of the nail lightly into the surface of the metal with the hammer. Use the #60 to #65 drill bits to put holes through the metal at precisely these marked points. Use a high speed and light pressure when drilling, because small drills break very easily.

5. Clamp the silver sheet onto the bench pin with a C-clamp, positioning the areas to be cut so they fall over the bench pin opening.

6. Remove the lower end of the jeweler's saw blade and insert it through one of the drilled holes. Refasten the blade and cut out the area, working slowly and carefully. The areas to be cut out will require frequent turning of the saw blade, so be prepared to cut slowly and to stop frequently.

7. Cut out each internal area (including the finger opening); then cut out the exterior outline of the ring. Remember to cut on the waste side of the design.

8. To finish the surfaces and edges of the ring, start by filing off any rough areas or burrs. Then sand the surfaces with silicon carbide paper, working from 280 to 320 grit, and follow this with emery paper in successively finer grits. Finish the small internal surfaces with jeweler's files or by cutting a thin strip of cloth-backed emery paper and using the jeweler's saw frame to hold it. Insert it into the internal design areas exactly as you would insert a jeweler's saw blade.

9. To finish the finger opening, saw a 2-inch slit into the end of the wooden dowel and use this as a support for successively finer carbide and emery papers. Insert and use the papers as shown in illustration B.

10. For a final polish, apply buffing compound (red jeweler's rouge) to the soft cloth and give all exposed surfaces a good rubbing. For an easy way to make an electric buffer from your electric drill, see page 16.

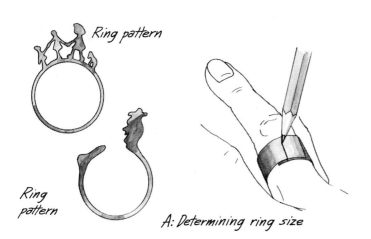

Ring pattern

Ring pattern

A: Determining ring size

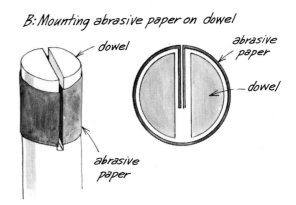

B: Mounting abrasive paper on dowel

dowel

abrasive paper

dowel

abrasive paper

Beads and Clay Ring

(Color photo on page 77)

Cut away at the back for easy fit, this cigar-band styled ring has both the massive good looks of a man's ring and the careful color harmonies of the most delicately enameled lady's ring. Made from commercially packaged plastic clay, the ring is flexible and lightweight; you'll soon forget you even have it on.

Equipment: Art knife, tissue paper, smooth glass or ceramic surface, small ruler, pencil, rolling pin or section of large-diameter wooden dowel, hatpin or other scribing tool.

Materials: One 2-inch-diameter ball of plastic clay as discussed on page 6, one package *each* of blue, magenta, and green commercial powdered cold-water fabric dye, one package *each* of brown and white Indian seed beads, jewelry cement.

How to Make

1. Divide the ball of clay in half and split one of the halves into thirds. Set aside the remaining half of the clay.

2. Open one packet of powdered dye and shake out a small amount onto the glass surface. Wearing rubber gloves, knead the powdered dye into one of the thirds of clay until it is well mixed. Add a few drops of water to the clay to bring out the brilliance of the dye color. Repeat for each of the two remaining thirds until you have three balls of clay in three different colors. Set the clay aside to dry for an hour or so at room temperature.

3. Trace the pattern given below onto tracing paper.

Roll out the ball of white clay until it is about 1/16 inch thick; then, using the art knife and ruler, trim out a 4-inch-long clay strip the width of the tissue paper pattern. Lay the clay strip on the glass, pressing lightly to adhere the strip to the glass.

4. Cut the tissue pattern apart into five separate pieces as indicated in pattern below. Roll out each of the colored clay balls to a thickness of $\frac{1}{16}$-inch. Press the cut-apart tissue patterns onto the surface of each of the colored clays and carefully cut them out. Lay the tissue and clay pieces in the proper order on the surface of the 4-inch strip of white clay ring pattern and gently press them into place. Carefully peel off tissue.

5. With the hatpin or scribing tool, mark the clay with the remaining dotted pattern lines as indicated below. When this has been done, press the seed beads into the clay, following the pattern below. Brown seed beads are used for the center and white seed beads for the outer parts of the design.

6. When all parts of the ring design are firmly pressed together, carefully peel the ring off the glass surface and size it by wrapping the band around your finger. Overlap both ends and cut through both layers with the art knife (illustration A), remove excess clay, and join the cut ends as shown in illustration B.

7. Bake the ring in a 325° oven for 20 minutes (use an old pie pan) until the clay is firm. When the ring has cooled, try it on. If it has shrunk and is too small, cut through it at center back; it will retain its shape.

8. Put a drop of clear jewelry cement over each bead to hold it in place; then coat the entire ring body with a thin layer of clear jewelry cement to strengthen it.

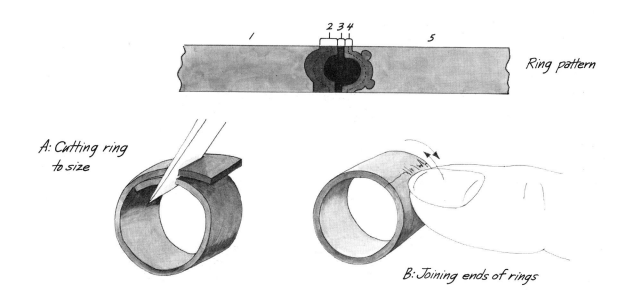

Ring pattern

A: Cutting ring to size

B: Joining ends of rings

Index

List of Jewelry Suppliers

Allcraft Tool and Supply Company
215 Park Avenue
Hicksville, New York 11801
(Findings, hardwoods, metals,
    stones, tools)

Anchor Tool and Supply Company,
    Inc.
12 John Street
New York, New York 10038
(Tools)

California Crafts Supply
1096 North Main Street
Orange, California 92667
(General crafts supply)

Craftool Company, Inc.
1421 West 240th Street
Harbor City, California 90710
(Lapidary equipment, tools)

T. B. Hagstoz and Son
709 Sansom Street
Philadelphia, Pennsylvania 19106
(Findings, metals, tools)

C. R. Hill Company
2734 West 11 Mile Road
Berkley, Michigan 48072
(Findings, metals, tools)

Swest Incorporated
10803 Composite Drive
Dallas, Texas 75220
(Findings, metals, tools)

Myron Toback, Inc.
23 West 47th Street
New York, New York 10036
(Findings, metals)